WRITERS REPUBLIC

PURPLE PASSION

THE INCLINATION OF THE RIGHTFUL SIN

WILTON ANTHONY ORR

WRITERS REPUBLIC L.L.C.
515 Summit Ave. Unit R1
Union City, NJ 07087, USA

Website: *www.writersrepublic.com*
Hotline: *1-877-656-6838*
Email: *info@writersrepublic.com*

Ordering Information:
Quantity sales. Special discounts are available on quantity purchases by corporations, associations, and others. For details, contact the publisher at the address above.

Library of Congress Control Number: 2023933134
ISBN-13:   979-8-88810-332-6   [Paperback Edition]
                  979-8-88810-333-3   [Digital Edition]

Rev. date: 02/16/2023

CONTENTS

YOU ARE MY EVERYTHING

You are my world.

Never in my wildest dream did I ever imagine such an amazing woman.

You are the apple of my eye, the sun that brightens my day, the star in my sky, the moon that shimmers throughout my night, the most stunning being in my universe.

You are my joy, my treasure, my world of laughter, my latest and greatest aspirations, my today, my tomorrow, my forever and a day.

You are not just my want but also my need, my personal drug that I can't do without.

You are the oxygen that keeps me alive.

With you my heart finds its beat.

You are the blood that flows through my vein.

You are my one and only.

For without you, I am but a shell.

You are my heaven and without you is hell.

You are the wind beneath my wings.

You are my strength, and without you I'm weak.

Before you came into my life, I was hopeless, lonely and incomplete.

When you showed up, I knew you were heavenly sent.

You make my life so beautiful, wonderful, and new.

I'm so in love with you.

FOR YOU ONLY

Tonight is a special night not just any night
Because you can have everything you want your way.
Just close your eyes and let me extract the sweet nectar
from your blossom.

Tonight let's leave the world behind
And let me take you to a place where only love resides.
I know all your secrets and all those sensitive places
to touch you that makes you shiver and shake
Till you scream and say you can't take no more.

When you are close to me
I hunger for you even more each time
Let me peel away your inhibitions
I will go nice and easy
I will go gentle and slow
I want your love so bad,
It makes my nature aches.

All day I've been waiting for the first chance
to explore your secret places
My passion burn inside
My desire intensifies and make me want
to take you to passion's highest peak.

Tonight I'll be the flame burning inside you
Right here, right now
I'll make all your fantasies come true
I got the answer to all the questions in your head
Even the ones you have not asked aloud
Let's make our love last the whole night through.

Give me every bit of you
I won't miss one lick or one stroke at your G-spot.

Tonight I'll keep you satisfied cause satisfaction is guaranteed
Baby, I'll bring down the lights
Bring down the music
It's gonna take hours before we are through
I can't make love that's only for a minute
I'll be inside of you as long as you want me to be
You are everything I ever wanted and everything I'll ever need
Tonight I'll be the freak between your sheets
Your satisfaction is guaranteed.

Thinking of you
That's all I seem to do
Without you is like ocean without wave.
I never want to spend a minute without you
You're on my mind each and every day
I think about you while I am on the job
I think about you when I lie down to bed
Reminiscing about you is the next best thing
to being with you
You're my sun on a cloudy day
You're my umbrella on a rainy day
You are to me, like coffee in the mornings,
a warm shower in winter,
deep meditation in times of sadness
You're my everything what can I say
There is nothing I would rather do,
than spend a lifetime making you my Queen
You deserve a husband, a crown and a throne
You're my number one and you're the best
You're like a tattoo in my mind that will never be erased
You are my life, you are my world,
Never did I imagine such amazing girl
I'll Love you forever because this isn't a phase.

Your succulent lips are like honey
Your kisses taste like wine
Intoxicatingly sweet, like heaven frozen in time
when I kiss you.

Your chocolate skin blend so very perfectly
It has no flaws nor imperfections.

Your body pose with a hill-flower grace
You're the embodiment of sexually and sensuality
A teaser in every sense of the word.

You shimmer like the morning mist
Your eyes are like previous gem stones, so beautiful
The chandelier are dancing in them.

My Angel!
My one true weakness!
My Queen!
You take my breath away.

Never has there been a girlfriend so fine
Sublime and splendid
So lustful and subliminal
the way you captivated me.

Your essence, your presence,
Your intelligence, your being and your soul,
Mesmerize and stunned me completely.

Logical explanations are genuinely not enough
To compare the beauty you possess.

You're a gift from the angels
They made you in heaven.

HER DIVINE BEAUTY

Face that mesmerize
A smile so engrossingly enticing
Captivating brown eyes
Stunning and seductive
With a progressive style
Makes you even more reflective.

Lips sweet as sugar
Upper so tender, lower so exquisite
So intoxicating
To kiss them I linger
They enslave me with grandeur.

Legs so thrill they beckon to kneel at the altar
Imprisoned wish I conceive, the way they
captivates and deceive
The unspoken words they whisper.

Your voluptuous body I adore
Skin so smooth and spotless
Please give me a tour
To explore and discover
The unforbidden hidden wonders
Swollen with desire
Thirsty for pleasure
Devoted by nature.

There's no telling what I will do the way
my body aches with hunger for you
An omnipotent flame of never-ending stupendous desire.

WIFE-TO-BE

You are the light of my life
The Joy of my heart
The center of my world
You're my all, you're my everything.

You captivated me with your presence
More dazzling than the stars
More stunning than the sun
More fabulous than the bubble
in a glass of champagne
More magnificent than the rainbow.

You intoxicated my soul with your smile
You cuteness knows no bounds
You beauty has no flaws
Your adorableness has no limits
I look at you and gasp in awe
You completely takes my breath away
Astonishing you are to me.

From the moment I saw you
I knew you were the one
I knowingly and willingly fall in love
with you on first sight
I promise to love you unselfishly always
Never will I break your heart.

Here's my heart unconditionally
No questions, no doubts, no insecurities,
You don't even have to think twice
About me making you my wife.

YOUR LOVE

Your love is such an indescribable blessing
It's rather wondrous and completely amazing,
especially different every time
Each day I spend with you is a wonderful surprise, happily excited
You're different and special in every way imaginable
You got me feeling like the breeze, soothing, easy and free
It gentle caresses my soul and move right through me
You give me the thrills; all my fantasies and dreams you richly fulfill
Every touch energizes and electrifies my body
Never did I imagine such contentment, deep
satisfaction and total fulfillment.

Mesmerized by your ebony beauty
You capture my heart from the start
Charming and graceful, enchanting and elegant,
amazing and innocent.
There is nothing else I would cherish more in life
You are all I ever wanted and everything I need
Like butterflies fan its wings gracefully in a lush garden
with nature's endowment to adorn
I too get excited when I think of being in your garden of paradise
Stupendous glory of nature's mystical endowment
an omnipotent flame of desire and the lust I must
You have the most gorgeous brown eyes
Every time I look in them, I'm lost in the reflecting glare
You have the most spotless chocolate skin complexion
and the neatest and sexiest curves body
Every time I imagine touching you
my hands tremble like earthquake
You have the most kissable pair of lips
Anticipating the intoxicating kiss that lies between them
Your long legs and perfect thighs
Can just imagine the sweetness that lies between them
It's everywhere I wanna be…
Not being able to
Damn, what a stress!!!!!!

MY LOVE

I'm sending you a love poem so you could know just how I feel
I have so much I want to tell you
But the right words won't come my way
No matter how hard I try.

I never tried before to use a poem to get my points across
Listen closely to each line
I hope lyrically it says what's on my mind.

I want you to know that you are thought of
every second of every day
You make me happy, you make me smile
You make my waiting worth the while
You are my richest treasure
You give me such long lasting pleasure
I hold tight to each amazing memory of you
Thinking how pleasurable and sweet it was the last time.

A special place I'll keep for you in my heart
For the life we had before we met, just seem do long ago.
Loving you is so wonderful, so precious, and so right.
Thinking about you is the next best thing to being with you
Just knowing and hearing that you care
with only words from your sweet lips,
relieves my pain whenever I am without your gentle touch
Even when we are apart, you never fail to lift my spirit
and brighten my day.

Like I've said so many times before
It makes no difference where you are
You could be here beside me or you could be miles afar

You and I share something very special

Something that feels so perfect
So right from the very beginning
That makes me believe in destiny
Perfect love, I call it
I could not ask for anything more
All I need to do is remember the all our times together
And look forward to all the time we have yet to come
And all the memories left for us to make
Je t'aime...

JAMAICA

Jamaica a country of little hope and few opportunities, where uncertainty lies ahead and good quality life seems almost impossible, where problems comes faster than a speeding bullet and more powerful than a locomotive.

A look in life's mirror only show the reflection of disappointment, failure, and more hardship. Our everyday reality seem a million miles away from the Spanish hotels and the sandy white beaches on the northern shores.

Quitting maybe the first thought that comes to mind when you working six days a week and for minimum wages that can't even buy food and just put us in the mood to surrender.

The very things that we pray for and try so hard to overcome seems unreachable.

Poverty, injustice, crime, and failure seems to be the order of the day. Poverty is one of the most common crime present throughout society, usually hidden by government and high-ranking officials through our athletes and tourism sector.

Where the relevant authorities pay little interest to the poor, and the people in the ghetto and tenement yards live in deplorable condition. After all the struggles and challenges throughout our lives, let's not be swayed by our temporary feelings, stretch out hand mentality, and/or the sweet promises of politics and vote because we have a right to but rather be convinced that the mindset of our leaders are in our best interest and the will power to persist and fight the good fight as long as there is a cause to be championed.

When we come to the end of our rope, don't let go tie a knot and hang on, because the determination and courage to persist will overcome any obstacles life throws at us,

We will prevail. We shall overcome.

Something is always happening. We don't always see them happening but are willing to accept them when they do. Life is like that. Sometimes they are great moments that you love to replay, and there are moments when you come face-to-face with life and reality at the same time. We find ourselves fearful of going forward and equally fearful of turning back. That's the sacrifices life puts up through sometimes. One moment we are walking through life's doorway full of hopes, dreams, goals, and opportunities; feeling good about who we are and where we need to be on a track of greatness and accomplishments, where society embraces us and people stood in lines to hear our good ideas. But as soon as we fail or make a mistake, the same persons who embrace our values, opinions, and ideas are the ones who abandon us. They see us as a failure but quick to hold up those with new ideas. We forget that they were the ones who taught us what we already knew. We seem to think that people must prove themselves to us again and again, and if we fail to live up to their expectations, we criticize, disrespect, and abandon them. We forget they were the ones who help us when we needed help, who taught us when we needed a lesson, who love us even when we were hard to love. Life is like that sometimes. Suddenly without warning, everything that we spend years trying to accomplish takes just seconds to tatter. We look around and see the same persons that we were quick to help turn their head on the other side and walk on by when everything inside us is crying out for help, a cry we fear no one can possible hear or understand. Along way down on every side, our courage fails. Instead of uplifting each other, we hang like lead weight, constantly pulling each other down. We fail to comfort the comforter in time of needs. We forget no one live or leave this world without someone else's intervention.

Breathtaking and stunning not a flower nor a portrait
Or the seven wonders of the world
More astonishing than anything my eyes have ever behold
My heart beats out of control, stunned and amazed
I'm dumbfounded every time I see you
Can't believe angels still exist here on earth
Not even the glow of dawn that points to the end
of the universe could create something so spectacular
Your crystal eyes so amazing
I just can't look away
They captivated me more than the magical mist of angels' falls
Charming, unbeatable, exquisite and adorable
Your beauty can never be quantified
It glows like the morning sun
Not even scientific methods can explain your remarkable beauty
From your hair follicles to your toenails,
there's just no logical explanation
here on earth because you were made in heaven
carefully handcrafted by God himself to perfection.

I lied not because I was guilty but because it was
the next best thing to being truthful.

Some say hard work is the key to success, but sometimes quitting is your only success.

Your ebony eyes have got me
They are so sweet and deep they drown me in
Intoxicated, I am lost by the soothing effect, they hide in them
Mesmerize, with uncontrollable love and emotion
Only for you I feel such devotion
Every time I look at you
I see the true beauty and promises of tomorrow
lying deep within your ebony eyes
Such vision of pure angelic each time I look at you
Your incomparable beauty melts my heart
like snow when the ray of sun is felt
Your full soft vanilla lips and the smell of your aromatic breathe
Anticipating the intoxicating kiss that lies between them
My heart shivered with excitement every time I picture kissing them
Those voluptuous legs and perfect thighs
Anticipating the sweetness that lies between them
Mystified by the benevolent, magnetism of your being
infuse my mind and melted my soul
Like an intoxicating remedy and the feel of tranquil serenity
I'm overwhelmed with obsessions
How I want to slowly undress u as I sigh!
With anticipation how I am gonna enjoy all of your heavenly delights
My goddess in high heels, temptress divine.

In my thoughts and in the center of my soul
I yearn to see you
My body aches with hunger for you
Imagining the next time I see you and the special smile
you save just for me
Oh how I pray God would guide you my way
I'm so head over heels in love with you
A moment with you would be pure bliss
Anticipating, you save the deepest and sweetest kiss
Just for me.

TIME FLIES

It's been a long time since I last saw your angelic face
It's amazing how every time I close my eyes
No matter what the season is or what time of day
It's your face that I see
Every time I speak, it's your voice I hear echoing
Through these tears that I'm crying
Reflect the hurt I can't control
I know we said our last goodbye
And at some point I have to move on
But before I do, I wanna know ask you one thing
Why did you leave me?

I won't quit on life because life never quits on me.

LIFE'S STRUGGLES

Some say it's too hard living
Others say hard work is the key to success
But neither sum up the real struggles of life
Some of us live from paycheck to paycheck
Others are living below the poverty line
While some are dying from hunger
Never has poor people struggles more real
Never has the cry for help trumpet louder
Struggling with challenges that continuously reappear
Constantly battling the iniquities of life
Only leave us submersed in despair
Fearful of what lies ahead and equally fearful of turning back
Along way down on every side
What tranquil serenity?
Like the rich and powerful on Wall Street
But the harsh reality of life's struggles on Harlem Street.

Look at us, we are inseparable
The way you look at me tells me we are such an adorable couple
The way you kiss me tells me we are undoubtedly meant to be
The way you hug me tells me we are unbreakable
The way you love me tells me what we share is incomparable.

I simply could not imagine
A more beautiful sight
I love everything about you especially that angelic smile!
Every time I look into your brown eyes
I see the reflection of the universe glittering
Like a telescope searching for distant stars
So beautiful and magical
You are such a remarkable reflection of pure natural angelic beauty
Such a pleasure to behold
I must be the luckiest man that has ever graced this earth
No other guy has been blessed so much
To have such an amazing woman as his wife/girlfriend
The day we met was so special, such a wonderful surprise
The moment I looked into your eyes
I knew that I had found my perfect future Queen
I promise to love you for every moment of forever
The way you kiss me takes my breath away
Your love warm me like the sun,
It heals my soul and brings me peace of mind
Waking up beside you in the morning is the best part of my day
Because when I'm with you I feel extraordinary
You illuminated my heart with happiness
Words just aren't enough to say
How much of indescribable blessing you are to me
You're one in a million, my most special one
I'm so blessed I found you as my priceless prize
I searched with the rest and discovered the best.

YOU ARE MY SOUL MATE

I'm connected to you completely, mentally, spiritually
At the same time incredible attracted to physically.
You're like my religion.
You bring so much joy to my heart and meaning to my life.

You truly capture my heart and soul.
Every day with you is filled with smiles and purpose.
I adore you. I love you.
You are my whole world—the stars, moon and sun.
Everything seems so right when I'm in your arms.
I wish to freeze every moment with you.

You are my forever Queen.
And I vow to love you always.
I never thought I would find such incomparable source of happiness.
Without you, I would cease to exist, have no reason to live.

I want the world to know how excited I am
To be in love with you.
Your presence is tangible to my touch
And I'm able to see you in my sight for as long as I live.
In you I find fulfillment and completeness.

There's nothing in the universe that compares to you.
Never for a moment imagine that I will stop loving you.
Every moment with you is Golden.
You are a beautiful Angel
Sent from the heavens above.
A treasure in every sense of the word.

YOU ARE MY STARSHIP

Come take me up tonight
I don't care where
It doesn't matter, as long as we are together
To the moon, whirling silently in space
If not, well, let's run away to England, Netherlands,
or even Disneyland
Wherever is fine by me
I just don't want to be away from you
Coz without you is like a colorless rainbow,
a starless night, a flameless fire
You are the sparkle that light up my universe
When I'm with you I feel so reassured
My heart is filled with joy because of your love
You are my one and only
I never want to lose you
I want to be your husband, and I want you to be my wife
I want to be with you for the rest of my life.

I think you are phenomenal, exceptional, sensational, spectacular and so much more! By far the most beautiful of God's creation, second to life itself. An angelic star is what you are. You shine so brightly, your shadow cast a silhouette so diverse that others are asking to barrow. My eyes have never been blessed to see something so pure and beautiful inside and out. You're such an unframed masterpiece. The purest sense of elegance and femininity. Your brown eyes sparkle like dew on a sunflower in the early morning.
Your lips are so desirable, only God could have made them just for that special someone. Your sexy walk like sprang in your hips, and the way your gracefulness completely takes my breath away.
You're perfectly curved body and purposeful gait, the way it holds my attention.
Your every nuance drives me crazy.
I'm so intoxicated by you.

From the soul of your femininity
To the silhouette image of you
Everything about you is naturally beautified
Flamboyantly, Tenacious, Vivacious,
Elegant and Graceful
Your whole being is beautiful
So errorless made in the heaven's above
I look at you and delightfully and lustfully
You are everything my mind, body and soul hungers for
Your temptation is the inclination of a rightful sin
If this indescribable feeling of love, lust,
Intimacy and vibe isn't the stairway to heaven
Hell is where I wanna be
Because you are the closest thing to heaven
Such blissful and insightful taste of nature's reality
The lust and desire I must
Like Eve in the Garden of Eden
You are my only demise
So wrong, yet feels so right
Oh what sinful act
I will burn in hell fire
The way you captivated and deceive me ostentatiously.

I never thought I could spend every second
Loving one person and find so much happiness it in
You are the best thing that has happened to me
You are the love of my life my soul mate,
my lifeline, my everything

No words can ever say, no feelings can ever express
How you make my life so beautiful, wonderful and new
You captured my heart and soul in one fell swoop
The true essence that is wonderful you
Every time I kiss your irresistible lips, I taste it
Every time I hug you, I feel it
Every time we made love, I full joy it

I love you with every ounce of my being
Will you be my wife?
No matter where I go or what I'm doing
You're always on my mind
I could never imagine a life without you!
Every day with you is a dream come true
I adored and celebrated every moment we spent together

For an eternity I will spend making you the happiest woman on earth
My life is yours, my hopes, my dreams and desire too
You are everything I could ever need and more
So much more than I deserve, prayed for and wish for

You are the most amazing, sweetest, kindest,
most caring person I ever met
I'm so lucky to have found you
My life is now complete in way I cannot express
But can only be felt with the heart
The true definition of beauty, joy, happiness,
friendship and everlasting love.

The beauty of life
Is that nothing protects the heart like patience
While we cannot undo what is done
We can learn from it, understand it, and change it
So don't give your doubts too much time
Don't allow your emotions to overpower your intelligence
Don't let your fear speak too loud
Don't be too surprised when people let you down
The truth is only a few people understand
What it means to truly be there for someone
And that's the saddest part about being on life's journey
Either someone decides to fight for you, or they do not
But at the end of the day you have to respect that
You have to realize there are certain things in life you cannot control
Some will only be there for you as much as the can use you
Your destiny is never tied to anyone who leaves you
It just means that their part in your journey comes to an end.

WONDERFULLY YOU

I have seen sunset that's nothing short of magical
But when I look at you, you defies all description known to mankind
I have seen the rain bow in all its magnificent colors
But nothing compare to the beauty I see when I look at you
I have seen the moon shine in all its diversity
But I'm yet to see anything as astonishing as you are
I have seen diamonds and pearls
Dazzle my eyes like dew on a sunflower early in the morning
But no matter what wonders my eyes have seen
There's just no comparison
To the beauty I see when I look at you
I have seen the seven wonders of the world
So beautiful, diverse and divine
But nothing is a breathtaking as you are
Your gracefulness roam the expanse of my mind
So much that I admire
So much I treasure and so much I cherish.

AMAZINGLY YOU

I never realize how routinely boring my life was
Until the day I met you
I never knew how enthralling a smile could be
Until you bestowed me with one
I feel so lucky because you are one-of-a-kind
And someone like you is impossible to find.
Some say there's no perfect person in this world
Yet from your hair follicles to the sole of your feet
Speaks of nothing but pure natural perfection
I never understood how intoxicating love could be
Until you showered me with love
I surely never thought how beautiful falling in love could be
Until I am completely head over heels for you.

THE GARDEN OF EDEN

Never saw a face as beautiful as yours
Never had a love as wonderful as yours
Your smile is amazing
Your kisses ablazing
Your lips so pure so sweet
I could go on and on...

When I first look in your eyes I knew
I could never love anybody but you
When you look at me never wonder
What's on my mind it's so plain to see
The answer's not hard to find
You are the reason I feel so alive.

Like an irresistible melody you capture my heart
Of all the woman in the world that I could be with
I wanna be with you most of all.

Like the Garden of Eden
Your temptation feel so right
If your love is not the stairway to heaven
Hell is where I wanna be.

When it come to you
Time is no better spent
A love that has been heavenly sent
It gives me everything
My heart need not to repent.

I love the way you love me
My heart is more than content
To keep you satisfied is my heart's birth consent.

YOU ARE MY EVERYTHING

You are my world
Never in my wildest dream did I ever imagine
such an amazing woman
You are the apple of my eye
The sun that brighten my day
The star in my sky
The moon that shimmers throughout my night
The most stunning being in my universe
You are my joy, my treasure, my world of laughter
My latest and greatest aspirations
My today, my tomorrow, my forever and a day
You are not just my want but also my need
My personal drug that I can't do without
You are the oxygen that keeps me alive
With you my heart finds its beat
You are the blood that flows through my vain
You are my one and only
For without you, I am but a shell
You are my heaven and without you is hell
You are the wind beneath my wings
You are my strength, and without you I'm weak
Before you came into my life, I was hopeless, lonely and incomplete
When you showed up, I knew you were heavenly sent
You make my life so beautiful, wonderful, and new
I'm so in love with you.

MY DESERT ROSE

You are beautiful and rare as a desert rose
It would say u are a looker from head to toes
You are funny, dainty, fragile and as feminine as can be
You are smart, adorable, charming, gorgeous, exquisite,
stunning, radiant, sexy, breathtaking, dazzling, delightful,
enchanting, irresistible, and lovely and everything to me
You are the apple of my eyes
The star in my sky the rainbow across my world
The most stunning being in my universe
You are my life
You are my world
Never did I ever imagine such an amazing woman
You make my heart beat fast
My knees quiver
You are the sexiest woman I had ever lay eyes on
You will be forever what I adore.
You are my comfort when I'm lonely
I was afraid and in your love I found peace of mind
You are my serenity when I need rest
It's you that gets me through tomorrow
Without you I am incomplete
Of all the woman I have known I must rate you the best
If there's one face I want to see
So beautiful, so pure, so true
One smile that makes a difference to everything I do
I'll have to say it's yours.

LOVING YOU

Loving you has made my life so beautiful
You bring out the best in me
Something no one else has been able to do
Something new that I never felt or dreamt of before.

You light up my world with sunshine and magic
Like a summer with a thousand Julys and fireflies filling my nights
With beautiful dreams, forever fulfilling my fantasies
And giving me the feeling that this is meant to be

You mean so much more to me than you will ever realize
So much more than I could ask for
So much more than the world can see
So much more than I thought my heart could ever feel
So much more than I thought I could show
So much more than my feelings can express.

You are everything I hope and prayed for and everything that I need
So sweet to know that we are a special pair
That goes beyond the changing of the season
I hope in return, I might have saved the best of me for you
One true and unselfish love
God's gift sent from above.

There's no definition fitting
Nor any limit nor beginning
Or end to your unfathomable beauty
It succeeded all of my known comprehension.

Your perfectly curves, it has no flaws,
no faults, no imperfection
Such an unframed masterpiece.

Your diversity is limitless and boundless
You're an idol of astonishingly philanthropic.

Your charming ebony eyes mesmerize
I loose myself in your enchanting stare
Your warming smile magnetized.

Your lips drips with chrome
Such a temptation to kiss
The insatiable magic of your appearance
The intoxicating smell of your breath
as sweet as a fully bloomed rose.

Within your soul, lies the heaven made for me
Within your heart, lies the love I've always sought
Within your eyes, lies all the beauty of the night.

I've known you for a little over a year
Yet it feels like I have known you for all my life
I can't hardly wait
Till I can finally be with you
You're so far away
I don't know what to do
I spend my days and nights
Thinking about you
I call you on the phone
You call me too
But it doesn't do justice
Nothing is more difficult than spending 24 hours
Without setting my eyes on you
Every moment with you is Golden
The happiness you bring my heart, no words can ever say
You are everything I could ever need and more
I can't hardly wait
When that day came, when I see you again
It seems like so long
Since I saw you last
Every day I am not with you
Is the opposite of fast?
I miss you so much
I've never felt more loved or more care for than
When you hold me, kiss me or tell me that you love me.

Some say the portrait of the Mona Lisa is stunningly beautiful
like a work of art
But your beauty surpass that of a Goddess
You are flawless and special in every way imaginable
From your hair follicles to your toenails
The masterpiece of brilliance just flows
It's as if you were handcrafted
By God's finest work of artistry
In his image of beauty and purity unimaginable to that of an angel
Your perfection soar to the heavens
By far the most gorgeous woman on planet earth.

You are flawlessly beautiful
By far the most gorgeous woman I ever laid my eyes on
You are the center of my attraction
One look at you set my soul on fire
Your unique style, personality,
class and gracefulness are unimaginable
Your perfection is unbelievable
You are like the heaven, so enticing in golden honor
I'm so enchanted by your diversity
The masterpiece of artistry
from your eyes, nose, curves, thighs, legs
all the way down to your toes
Captivated by their unspoken words.

Your smile is incomparable
Your touch is insatiable
Your vibe is just incredible
Your beauty is indescribable
You are a heavenly design!!
I am completely stunned by neatness of your perfection.
These are just some of the reasons why my mind go crazy
When I hear the sound of your angelic voice
My hands tremble like earthquake
When I imagine touching your beautiful face
My ego soars and my heart aches
When I think of your irresistible lips touching mine
I know I'm yours truly and completely.

UNIQUELY YOU

I've been to so many places
I've seen so many faces
Asians, Blacks, Hispanics, White and Indians
But never saw a face as beautiful as yours
No matter what wonders my eyes have seen
Nothing is as delectable as you
Your smile is amazing
Your skin soaks with shea butter so soft and beautiful
Your long sexy legs spread like the wings of a flyer
The way you sway those indulging thighs like spring in your hips
Got my eyes stuck on you
Like a hillside petals, no other flower could compare
The image of you is so breathtaking
Like the reflection of heaven frozen in time
I have never seen anything so astonishing
You are a goddess
A gift from the heavens
You are what I've been searching for
Hoping to find
Chasing after
Just a glimpse of you knocks me off my feet
and have my heart beating in turbo speed
Imagining just a sip of your pink lips
Like selective wine of distinction,
flavored with delight distinguishing as lustful
The essence that is wonderfully you
Like a rose lost in the forest, graceful, triumphant, and wild
That excite a man's desires
Like an addictive drug that makes me only wants to get higher
So irresistible, hypnotizing and captivating
You got me trapped in a box of ponder
I wanna discover and explore all your hidden wonders.

The sight of you fill my eyes with so much lust and admiration
I have never seen anything so blissful and delightfully tempting

My sinful and lustful greed
A ravishing blaze of iridescent fire
This unquenchable thirst
Oh this craving
This yearning
This aching
This hunger
This longings
This feeling

You are as stunning as a rose lost in the forest
Graceful, beautiful, elegant, triumphant, and wild
Poised so gracefully like a hill-flower petals
Such an untamed beauty
Everything about you is splendid
The magic of your appearance completely
takes my breath away

You shimmer like a morning mist
Your eyes are like the darkest night,
adorned with a myriad
Lips so sweet they glazed with nectar
Your voice are like thrumming embers so irresistible
Your sinuous body making my heart sing,
harmonies of pleasure so divine
Your laughter harmonizes with the pulses of the universe

An exquisite blend of exotic beauty
Seductive and alluring
Indescribable, untranscribable and imbibable
Like heaven's zone glistening

Everything about you is amazing
So refreshingly beautiful inside and out.

Poverty is a poor man's crime, and wealth is a rich man's curse.

REMEMBERING YOU

Lying here thinking of you
From dusk to the dawning of the tropical sunrise
You are forever on my mind.
Feeling so lonely and insecure
Wondering if you're still mine
Or have you start to lose your love for me
The thoughts of you lying in bed
Wrapped in the arms of another lover
Makes my heart ache with pain
Certain death will come from this strain.
I hate the goodbyes
Wondering if there's anything I could have said
Like beg you to stay knowing that all my dignity
went away when you left
I wish you were still here
I miss you more and more each day
There is so much we haven't done
I know I will see you again
Life is so meaningless without you by my side
Because you're all that I am living for
I am slowing counting down the days
When I next see you
Because in your arms is where I long to be.

UNIQUELY YOU

Some says perfection is unattainable
When I look at you
Your perfection is undeniable
Like the Garden of Eden
In all its splendor
You dazzle me with glow
Your timeless and limitless beauty
Shines in every dimension
From head to toes
From hips to thighs
From eyes to nose
Both inside and outside
Your radiance and
Brilliance overflow.

MY LOVE FOR YOU

Flowers may bloom in spring
Tree leaves may turn golden in autumn
Snow may covered the streets in winter
Sunshine may sparkle in the summer
The seasons may change
Like a picture in a frame
But nothing will ever change
My love for you.

IN YOU

In your eyes I can see
The dreams of my reflection
In your smile I can see
The beauty that cannot be described
In your approach I can see
The solution to all my problems
In your arms
I find trust and comfort
In your care I find
The answer to all my questions
In your dreams I can hear
The sound of sweet heavenly bliss
In your heart
I find true love and happiness
In the silence of the night
I can hear you say
I love you
Even from miles afar.

THINKING OF YOU

Thinking of you that's all I seems to do
When you're not here
I long to hold you near
Without you is nothing more than fantasy
It's like ice cream without the cone
Time has made me see just what it means
to have you in my life
Someone that's true
My love belongs to you
There's no better one for me than you
When I close my eyes
I can still see your smile
It's so bright
It lights up my life
And guide me even out of my darkest hour
The happiness I found with you
Means more than you could ever know
More than you'll ever see
So much more than my heart could ever shows
It seems like every time I am with you
You does something incredible amazing
That leaves some unforgettable memories behind
That's why I carry
Thoughts of you wherever I go
Because they never fail to add their magic to my day.

I have been to all 54 states
I have seen so many beautiful faces
But I have never seen anything so astonishing
You test every limits of humanity
My eyes have the pleasure just to behold
Such remarkable beauty here on earth
Your diversity is boundless and limitless
You are the geographical wonder of science
Your stunning looks defy all known comprehension
There is just no definition fitting or comparison
to the unfathomable beauty you posses
It has exceeded all known English vocabularies
Your outer finesse surpassed every imagination
in the windmills of my mind
It has no flaws, no faults nor imperfections
Such flawless image only seen in beauty magazine
Incomprehensible one woman
Having everything from her hair follicles
All the way down to her toenails
Such an unframed portrait
A priceless possession in every sense of the word.

I LOVE YOU JUST THE WAY YOU ARE

You may not be as beautiful as the portrait of the Mona Lisa
But your inner beauty
Goes beyond what people see on your outer finesse
You may not have luminous silk hair on your shoulders
But I love yours
It's curly, short and neat
You may not have designer clothes, silk robes and fishnet pantyhose
But I love how your dress holds you, envelops you, outline your body
It compliments your unique, shape and style
You may not have gorgeous blue eyes
But your eyes are as beautiful as crystal-clear blue waters
Every time I look in them I'm completely lost in you whom
I absolutely adored
You may not have angelic voice
But when you call my name
Oh so sweet
You melt my heart without a heat
You may not have hourglass figure, voluptuous legs and perfect thighs
But I love the way how your body was design
Neat and sexy
You may not have flat stomach
Like Pulse models
But I love your little belly
It's living proof of the adorable son you gave me
Ha! Like they say beauty is in the eyes of the beholder
Perfection just doesn't exist
What can I say?
I love you just the way you are.

I admire you so much
Even this writer can't find the words
To tell you how much I love you
The epitome of gorgeous
Your beauty knows no bounds
Your adorableness has no limit
You are beyond cute
You're the only girl in the world that I will ever commit.
I gaze at you and gasp in awe!
Wondering how you're possibly mine.
The grace of your style
Takes my breath away effortlessly
And leave me speechless
Never has there been a girlfriend so fine
And never did I imagine I'd find, a girlfriend so perfect and kind
You gracefulness is comparable to the heaven's above
They say art is an expression of imagination
Then I guess you are an unframed masterpiece
A an embodiment of perfection
The moment you came into my life was a miracle.
I can't help but bless the day I met you every single day.
You are the best thing in my life
My muse and inspiration
You exceed all expectations
A gift from the heavens
You illuminated my soul with happiness.

MISSING YOU

When I am with you time flies by so fast
It's like the present is the past
I wish the time would stand still
So I could spend forever with you
It's almost a month since you've been away
Yet it feels like a year
The thoughts of you surround me
Everything seems so right when I'm in your arms
There is just no substitute for you
Even in the still of darkness
My heart, my body, my soul, misses your presence
When the first rays of sunlight
Spill like a waterfall between the blinds
The loneliness of you not being here creeps in
The thoughts of your smile, your laughter, and your company
Create a feeling that is impossible to express with words
I miss your sweet, soft lips
And the feel of your aromatic breathe on my face when we kiss
I miss your gentle hugs and the insatiable feeling
of your body touching mine
I miss our Sunday evening walks together
I miss us eating out once a week
Nothing in life before we met means this much
You are a true gift of beauty, joy, happiness,
friendship and everlasting love
And that's a feeling neither time, nor distance will ever change.

THE GARDEN OF EDEN

Never saw a face as beautiful as yours
Never had a love as wonderful as yours
Your smile is amazing
Your kisses blazing
Your lips so pure so sweet
I could go on and on
The first time I look in your eyes
I knew I could never love anybody but you
When you look at me never wonder
What's on my mind?
It's so plain to see
The answer's not hard to find.
You are the reason I feel so alive
Like an irresistible melody you capture my heart
Of all the woman in the world that I could be with
I wanna be with you most of all
Like the Garden of Eden your temptation feel so right
If your love is not the stair way to heaven
Hell is where I wanna be.
When it come to you time is no better spent
A love that has been heavenly sent
It gives me everything
My heart need not to repent
I love the way you love me
My heart is more than content
To keep you satisfied is my heart's birth consent.

I have been to all 14 parishes
I have seen so many beautiful faces
But I have never seen anything so astonishing
You test every limits of humanity
My eyes have the pleasure just to behold
Such remarkable beauty here on earth
Your diversity is boundless and limitless
You are the geographical wonder of science
Your stunning looks defy all known comprehension
There is just no definition fitting or comparison
To the unfathomable beauty you posses
It has exceeded all known English vocabularies
Your outer finesse surpassed every imagination
In the windmills of my mind
It has no flaws, no faults nor imperfections
Such flawless image are only found in beauty magazine
Incomprehensible
One woman having everything from her hair follicles
All the way down to her toenails
Such an unframed portrait
A priceless possession in every sense of the word.

Life never seems to be the way we want it
Some days I amaze myself
Other days I can't even find my own reflection in the mirror
However my current situation is not my destination
I'm constantly working on a better version of myself every day
I'm too focused to be doubtful
Way too ambitious to be fearful
Too positive not to be hopeful
And way too strong to be defeated.

I'm focus but equally confused
I'm happy but equally sad
I'm determined but equally fearful
I'm strong but equally weak
I'm hopeful but equally doubtful
It's too hard living yet I'm afraid not to try.

Our love isn't just anything or something
What we have is beyond comparison
You are the most precious thing I've ever been given
There will never be enough words to describe
just how much I love you
You are not just anyone or someone
You are the most amazing, sweetest,
most caring person I have ever met
You're undoubtedly my heart's greatest delight
Every time I look in your eyes I see it
My present and my future
You are in my dreams at night
And my thoughts throughout the day
I never thought I could love someone
in every single way.

You are the artistry of your own destiny
What you paint
Will be a reflection of how you see yourself
And will ultimately determine your future.

Life has its advantages and disadvantages
Perfection doesn't comes without failures
Don't be afraid to take chances
Neither let your fear speak too loud
You will never succeed your full potential
Until you find your true passion.

Sometimes life is like a dark and stormy night
Where so many uncertainty lies ahead
But when the storm is over
The sun rises and it becomes a beautiful day
It washes away the unnecessary doubts.

If I have to realize it,
I would say I can't live without.
You are the most precious thing I've ever been given.
If I have to characterize it,
I would say you are like a never-ending holiday.
Everything I want to celebrate.
If I have to summarize it,
I would say you are unforgettable in every way imaginable.
If I have to emphasize it,
I would say you are the most amazing, sweetest, charming,
smartest and caring person I ever met.
If I have to specialize it,
I would say you are like my favorite subject.
I wanna know everything about you.
If I have to prioritize it,
I would say you are like my passion.
Everything I want to pursue, explore and discover.
If I have to categorize it,
I would say you are the most beautiful thing God have ever created.
You are an angel in disguise.
If I have to finalize it,
I would say you are my everything.
My present and my future.

Don't give your doubts too much time
That you miss out on life's endless possibilities.

I see my struggles as an opportunity to survive things
And not as an adversity that can't be overcome
I see my struggles as an opportunity to fix things
And not as a barrier I can't get over
I see my struggles as an opportunity to grow from things
And not as an obstacle to keep me down
I see my struggles as an opportunity to try new things
And not as difficulties to keep me back
I see my struggles as an opportunity to change things
In the end life is like a photo shoot
You develop from the negatives.

WOMAN OF ELEGANCE

You are everything my eyes 👀 were meant to see
They are stuck on you like a TV screen
Captivated by your angelic beauty in every scene
You deserve an Oscar Award for being the most beautiful
Incomparable you are to mortals
Only heaven's angel could compared
You are definitely my object of perfection
The sexiness you display
The glow of your skin rivals the marvels of the universe
The span of your hips
The sun of your beaming smile
The confident in your style
The freedom in your naturality
Your body is the destination every eyes wants to land
The sight of you fills me with serenity
You are the archetype of gorgeousness
Not a single blemish have I seen in your frame
In every inch, perfection is sustained
You are the reflection of the Creator's blueprint
Purity in every form
Angel Queen of delight
You truly are the most beautiful
God's crowning achievement
Men fall down on their knees
Never has such remarkable beauty foreseen here on earth
Your outer finesse has experienced more curves
than round brilliant diamond
Your whole being is beautiful
Envied by woman…coveted by man.

You are so special to me
Words cannot express
The indescribable joy and happiness you bring
My feelings for you have grown stronger,
The chemistry we share is amazing
A feeling so sincere, a bond so strong
I can't deny how much I truly love you
I'm sure you never realize
You've been my will to live
You are the keeper of my dreams
The woman who holds my heart
You've shown me what it's worth
To love someone each and every day
Nothing is more exciting than spending
every precious moment with you
Everything you are
I'm not
You are the warming glow that brings my heart abloom
The serenity that you brings give me
peace of mind and tranquility
The strength that cannot be broken
The joy in my spirit
The happiness in my heart
What I feel for you is greater than love itself
Many are my favorite things,
But nothing is more precious than you are to me
Heaven knows that's a fact I cannot deny
Purity in your heart confirming that you are heavenly sent
You really makes me understand the truth of his Grace
You will never understand just how amazing you are
Meeting you gave me courage of higher degree
A love like yours I never thought I would find.

ABOUT LIFE

If I walk a perfect line, there will be someone to say I am too perfect
Even if I walk on water heaters, will say I'm blowing up dust
You could lie down for people to walk on
And they will still complain you're not flat enough
They just want reasons to complain and excuses to avoid
There are occasionally, every now and then,
Sometimes too often, people in our lives whom we just can't please.
Whatever and everything we do is wrong
Whatever we say is arguable or offensive
When we get on a really difficult track and have opinions
contrary to those of someone that doesn't appreciate us
We are branded as troublemakers, vagrants
We have a leadership problem
But it will take strong minds and a sensitive, nurturing spirit
to keep out all the negative voices
Throughout our whole lives we are doubted, we are criticized
and we are challenged
We have to learn how to steel ourselves against all the voices
that want to pull us down or to mislead us
and there are so many of them
When we fill our minds with positive thoughts
we leave no room for the uncaring ones
that strive to hurt us
So don't allow yourself to be easily fooled or discourage,
When you allow negativity a frequent journey
to your thoughts without paying a toll, remember,
you are on a track to disappointment and failure.

LOVE DON'T LOVE ME

Some say falling in love is the most beautiful thing
Others say love is infectious
You cannot pour it on others without getting
A few drops on yourself
But I wish I could say the same for you
Oh how you play me
You use me
You deceive me
You drained my very soul
Love, how you deprived me of you
And left me broken
For so long I have searched
Looking for you
Reminiscing how you gonna fill my heart
With happiness and leave me speechless
But in my quest to find you
Like a cold-blooded killer
You exceed all expectations of cruelty
You took the very heart of me
Goodbye, love
You have cost me too much!
How can something so beautiful bring
So much pain and sadness?
You have rob me of my innocence
You have blinded me
From finding my soul mate
Only left me broken hearted
And with shattered dreams.
Goodbye, love
You cost me too much!

Every time I look at you
You look like something magically delicious
Like a wet and juicy fruit that would just melt in my mouth
With sweetness and capture my senses in rhapsody
You are the perfect blend of sweetness
From head to toes
You are my strawberry sundae
I can't wait to hold you, touch you, lick you, kiss you,
caress you, explore you and drown in all your splendor
Only you and everything that you possesses will satisfy
my insatiable unfulfilled hunger of my sexual appetite
I crave your sweetness.

When it comes to you
Everything comes so naturally
Everything flows so effortlessly
Everything about you
Eloquently amazes me.

A love that grows immensely
A love that cannot be hidden
A feeling that burns, deep inside
Each day I ponder
Amazed I wonder
How truly and completely amazing
you are in every single way
Your sight makes me giddy headed
Irresistible to adore
Your love has captured me
My heart beats and my soul freezes
with every breath
My thoughts are shaped around you
Loving you is not a choice
It's my passion
You are the key to my heart
You are the best thing in my life
You have brought such an indescribable
and wondrous blessings
You have shown me true love that
I have never experienced.

MY AMERICAN QUEEN

You are like a calming Southern California wind
That gentle caresses and move right through me
Your smile is like a ripple of energy that illuminates my heart
Your gorgeous blue eyes sparkle like the deepest seas
Your lips are like nectar to me
Your kiss energizes my soul
You walk in such beauty
Like the stars gliding across the night sky
Like the city that never sleeps
Your sexiness is always on duty
The whole of your body is perfectly adorn
The way your every movement holds my attention
The way your every nuance drives me crazy
So many other men swarm around you
Like a hive of honeybees
For you are dazzling…mesmerizing…hypnotizing
You are golden, shine brilliantly like the sun
The rainbow envy the sight of your gracefulness
Even angels congregate around you
So that they can reflect the glow of your beauty
You are truly an American Queen
Bless with everything to spare
You deserve a ring, a crown and a thrown.

ALWAYS ON MY MIND

In your thoughts is where I want to be
When you close your eyes
I want to be the one you're thinking of
My mind go crazy when I don't hear from you
And even when we are apart
Your voice moves me and brings me tears of Joy
A sound I've never before known
Thinking about you makes me constantly smile
Something deep inside tells me you are the one
There is nobody I would rather have by my side
Because there is nothing more wonderful
Than having you here in my arms
I would do anything just to be with you
Each day and night you prove my life worth while
I appreciate you so much
You're someone I adore
This insatiable feeling of you is so incredible
I want it to hold me captive eternally
I carry your heart with me, so deep inside forever
Anywhere I go, you will go too
How amazingly sweet is that
You are always warm and cherished here in my heart.

BEAUTIFUL JAMAICAN WOMEN

You are like a calming southern wind
That gentle caresses and move right through me
Your smile is like a ripple of energy that illuminates my heart
Your gorgeous brown eyes sparkle like the blue mountain spring
The glow of your skin reflects a Caribbean sunshine
Your lips are like nectar to me
Your kiss energizes my soul
You walk in such beauty
Like the stars gliding across the night sky
Like the city that never sleeps
Your sexiness is always on duty
The plumpness of your breast
Roundness of your ass
The whole of your body is perfectly adorned
The way your every movement holds my attention
The way your every nuance drives me crazy
So many other men swarm around you
Like a hive of honeybees
For you are dazzling…mesmerizing…hypnotizing
You are golden, immaculately beautiful
The rainbow envy the sight of your gracefulness
Even angels congregate around you
So that they can reflect the glow of your beauty
You are truly a Jamaican Queen
Skin of black diamond and heart of gold
A strong Black woman beyond definition
Bless with everything to spare
You deserve a ring, a crown and a thrown.

MY HEART

The book of my heart belongs to you
You have written happiness in all its pages
No color of ray shines brighter
Than the color of you love
It fills my heart and soothes my soul.

Whenever I'm lonely and depressed
Just the thought of you make me whole
You are my inspiration
The strength of my life that cannot be broken.

You remind me that no matter what I do or fail to do,
There's still hope as long as I have faith in you.

When my day seems hopeless
You always say the things
To get me back on a focused track.

For the times when we are apart
I never fail to keep holding on
To every amazing dream of you.

For I spend so many quiet moments
Of my own thinking of how much I miss you
And how hard it is to be apart.

Every now and again I quietly close my eyes
And imagine you here smiling
Thinking such wonderful thoughts of you.

I don't know what magic makes people as wonderful as you

And how wonderful it is that you're always with me
Warm and cherished here in my heart.

JUST FOR YOU

Yearning for your presence
My body aches with hunger for you
You have all my senses smile in awe!
One look at you set my soul on fire
Oh, how I pray God would guide you my way
I'm head over heels crazy about you
Wish I could form my feelings into articulate words
Of love and wonder
And tell you of my aspiration
To be held sincerely in your arms,
where I need to be
Cuddling with you and just basking
In the sweet resonance of stillness
But I know that wish is unattainable
Far out of reach, yet I admire you still
Visualizing your immaculate beauty
My body shivered with bliss
How I slowly wanna undress you
As I sigh! With anticipation, so happily excited
How I'm gonna enjoy all your heavenly delights.
And even though I can't have you in person
Desires like these are true for you
Images of your behind still danced in my mind
Swollen with desire
Thirsty for pleasure
Devoted by nature
My immense desire and feelings for you is overwhelming
You got my feeling hot like an oven clock
at 360 degrees Celsius
Your only true crime is my intense hunger
and deep yearnings unfulfilled

Yet I adore the insatiable thrills of you
Anticipating the stunning feel of your body next to mine.

MY LOVE

There are no words to describe how I feel about you
I love you more than you'll ever know
In numberless forms and numberless ways
Being in love with you makes my heart sings
and life is worth living
You may think you're one of millions
but you're one in a million to me
You bring me joy so immense
I can barely utter a word
Completely dumbfounded
You've made me feel what I haven't felt before
Loved and appreciated
I promise to love you unselfishly always
Never will I break your heart
And never will we drift apart
Thank you for keeping it real
Showing me others were just playing
the role of a great pretender
No matter where I go or what I do
I'm thinking of you
To the world you maybe one person
but to me you are my universe
For so long I dream of the perfect girl
And now I realize it's you
But you're so much more than I imagined
I fell in love with you yesterday
And I will love you so much more today
I need you tomorrow, next week, next month, next year
and for the rest of my life.

PLUS SIZE

Beautiful plus-size women
Blacks, Caucasian, White, Hispanic, and Asian
Well-rounded, fluffy, thick, voluptuous
and full figured
Take a glance and be amused
The sun of your smile
The glow of your skin
The grace of your style
Phenomenal woman that's you
Sexy, thick, beautiful and proud
Such diversity in your variety
Exquisitely curved
You don't need sexy lingerie
or fishnet pantyhose
To attracts a man's attention
You are naturally beautified
Bless with everything to spare
From your hair follicles to the sole of your feet
You make all my senses smile in awe!
The span of your hips
The curl of your lips
The swing of your waist
And the joy in your feet
The inner mystery hidden between your thighs
Like soul food
You satisfied both body and mind
My deep yearnings nourished
And hunger fulfilled
The integrity of a great woman
By far the most attractive
From your curvaceousness,

Full breast, hips and thighs
Your sexiness can never be denied
The way you walk
Like you got gold mine hidden
between your indulging thighs
As you swing your hips from side to side
I realize why God created my eyes
It's you
The way your dress holds you, envelopes you,
imprint you, teases your skin like the wind
The harmonious movement of your feet
Got my attention like a deer trapped in a car's headlights
Never has there been a voluptuous full-figured woman so fine
Not even an eclipse could blinded me from such gracefulness
You are everything I wanna own and crown
You deserve a throne
Phenomenal woman that's you
Bold, fluffy, beautiful and proud.

SELF-AFFIRMATION

Nurture self-love
Seeking perfection
When there isn't a formula for it
Will only create doubts and fear
The beauty of life is being true to yourself
And proud of what makes you unique
Don't let other people opinion define you
Neither let others write your script
The moral of your story will be nothing more
than what they perceive you to be
When people can't put you in a box
They can't control your journey or value
You are the director of your own big screen
What you film will ultimately determine
your success story
There are endless possibilities and opportunities
to create your own masterpiece
Don't let others limit your potential
Believe in your self
Challenge orthodoxy because the will power
to persist lies within you
You never too old to hit the box office
and set new records.

I LOVE YOU

Never did I imagine I'd find a girlfriend
So gorgeous and kind
I never thought I could spend
Every second loving her
And find complete happiness in it
Every day with her is a wonderful surprise
Especially different every time
I love her more than life itself
I treasure her more than the air I breathe
I dream of her endlessly
I care about her more than
Anything in this world
I cherish her tirelessly
They say a good woman
Is a gift from the heavens
They say it's a blessing
They say it's a miracle
And I believe that it is
Because you are special in every single way
I vow to love you in all your forms
Today, tomorrow, next week,
next month, next year and forever
Love is a choice I've made to devote my life
To love you beyond your flaws, faults
and imperfections
You are the best part of my life
Your unwavering support elevated and empower
This once broken guy into a wholesome man
You were the missing puzzle of my life
The flame of love that brighten my universe
Everything about you is incredible and amazing

You've shown me what it's worth
To love someone each and every day
You are all the woman I need
No words can fully capture
How much I truly love you.

ALWAYS AND FOREVER

My thoughts of you yesterday was warm and sweet
And the day before that was incredible
And today my thoughts of you is splendid and beautiful
A matter of fact I am thinking of you right now
Reminiscing about the last time we were together
Thinking such wonderful thoughts of you
And how thankful I am to have you in my life
Can't believe I have such an remarkable woman in my life
A matter of fact what I really wanted to say
My whole world revolves around you
You are my universe
You makes every day such a joy to live
You are such an indescribable blessing
You captivated my heart and mesmerize my soul more
Than the seven wonders of the world
I look at you and all I can do is smile in awe!
Completely stunned and carried away
By your magnificence and diversity
Your beauty outshines the heavens above
I have never seen anything so naturally beautified
Such a marvelous reflection of poignant empathy
You have always been the best part of my life
My source of happiness,
Friendship, companionship, joy, love, comfort
Boo, you are not only the love of my life
But you are my life, my reality, my today,
My tomorrow and my future
My forever and always
I have never love anyone the way I love you
Can't even comprehend the fact that
I have always been in love with you.

COLORS OF AFRICA

Beautiful girls of color
Such an enigmatic beauty to behold
Empress of Jamaica
To the mothers of Africa
Black, beautiful and proud
Rock your dreadlocks, Afro or cornrows
Weather short, nappy, long or curly
Your true beauty lies in your naturality

Such splendid nature of your different shades of Black
Weather dark, light, or mixed racial
Your skin, your hair and your soul are beautiful
There is power in your youth and strength in your diversity

You have been gracefully infused with magic
Beautiful, strong, intelligent and independent
I'm Black, beautiful and proud
Boldness with a purpose

The glow of your skin
Soft like shea butter and rich as coffee beans
Naturally beautified
Beyond all definition
Still defying place and time and all expectations

Skin of chocolate and heart of gold
Beautiful Black girls
Lift your heads to the sky
Step right up in time
It's your time to shine
Take a full stride

Your place in history
Can never be denied
You demand the attention of the entire world

Take a glance and be amused
Just how phenomenal you are
Young women of elegance and class
You are definitely a credit to your Black race
I can see the reflection of Mama Africa
in your courageousness

My little Black princesses
Let them look and be aware that all Black girls are rare
Nothing compared to your glorious shades of melanin
Black girls you are truly a beautiful sight
You've brought beauty to the world
Children of Africa
You're a magical wonder.

INDIVIDUALISM

In a world where everyone is for themselves
Individualism doctrine is always at one's forefront
They tell you to live for yourself only
Don't expect anything from anyone
because expectations only hurts
We forget that no one live or leave this world
without someone else's intervention
But we pay little attention to we or us
Everything is about me, myself and I
And the sad thing is that
In the interval between Life and Death,
We are constantly fighting for what we did not bring
And for what we will not take
We need to realize that
There'll always be those who are greater,
more talented, more successful, and more famous
And there'll always be those who are less fortunate,
less successful, and poorer than us
So embrace your unique journey, regardless of your circumstances
Because you will never find your true purpose
or fulfill your potential if you only live for yourself.

LOVE

Love is not just anything or something
But can only be felt with the heart
They say it's a river that circles the earth
A bean of light shining to the end of the universe
Some say it's the most beautiful thing
It's a blessing
It's a gift and a miracle
Others say love is like a perfume
U cannot pour on others without getting
A few drops on your self
But whichever way it finds you
It changes everything
Love can protect your heart like patience
But also can wreck your soul like sin
So don't get your hopes up too fast
Neither give your doubts too much time
Love is like a game of chess
Sometimes you win
Sometimes you lose
But it ultimately comes down to how you deal
With your lost or your gain
You can either let it be an obstacle to keep u
Down, sad, empty, hurt and broken
Or an opportunity to explore new thoughts, new memories,
New feelings and endlessly possibilities.

LIFE

The road to success is full of setbacks
The future is surrounded by clouds of uncertainty
So invested in living each day
Your stock will increase overtime
Every decision we make has significance
So view life as a long-term investment
Stay commented to your principles and ideals
Focus on your direction
Life is a struggle and an endless fight
The greatest victory and accomplishment in life
Is the essence of living in this complex world
Never take anything for granted
Cherish every moment
Universal destiny is granted to us
for a limited span of time
Validity of our life's visa can be cancelled at any time
So make the best of today
Every new day is an opportunity
To become a better version of yourself
Eventually, you'll soar up to the sky
You have to remember
Even some birds can't fly.

REALITY

Life is like a season of changes
Like the weather it's totally unpredictable
So are the days of our lives
Fill with uncertainty of tides
Don't give your failure too much time
Nor let your fear overpowers
Your strength and determination
Even the driest desert on earth
Celebrate the abundance of life
When it rains
So the struggles you are experiencing
now is preparing you for growth tomorrow
Don't give your doubts too much time
Your beliefs, your attitude, your thoughts,
and your perspective
Will eventually shape your direction
The more enthusiastic you are about life
The better equip you are to rise above adversity.

ANTICIPATION

Things never look clearer
Happiness never seems nearer
From the moment I saw you
I knew you were the one!
How on earth do I get so lucky??
For so long I had searched
Looking for true love
And then one day out of the blue I met you
I spend days, weeks anticipating
When I will see you again
You got me feeling like a child on Christmas Day
Happily excited
How emotions have taken over me
As I anxiously await for us to go out on our first date
Reminiscing of us two going for a walk
Holding each other hands or just sitting in the park
Basking in the moment of something magical and new
It's true that every beautiful and perfect gifts
Comes from above.
You will forever what I adore
Like a special occasion
You're everything I want to celebrate here on earth.

LIFE SEASONS

Like a flower in bloom
Like the kiss of spring
Like the river flows in harmony
Like a dawning sunshine
Like a sunset bright orange glow
Like the wave that breaks ashore
Like a soothing Caribbean breeze
Like crystal clear blue water
To a magical sunset
Your love speak a thousand words
To which no price can be met.
Incredible is the feeling
Beautiful, precious, wonderful, so consistent
Don't stop it
Just keep it flowing
Today, Tomorrow and Forever.

IN BLOOM

You are the flower in bloom the bees never misses
The garden of paradise butterfly never misses
The blossom hummingbirds constantly hoovering
To taste its delicious nectar
Your exquisite beauty so serene
Even angels would fall
Never has such perfect beauty foreseen here on earth
A goddess is what you are
Even the most talented artist would struggle
To paint such flawless imagery
Your perfectly shape body were sculptured by God
And will be revered as one of God's finest work of art
Immeasurable, infinite, you are a goddess of beauty
Bless with tranquility and purity.
Your immaculate beauty outshines all
And I will dare and compare you to the heavens.
You're unique in the way that your essence radiates
And have the most astounding effect on all
By far the most amazing woman on planet earth
An angel in disguise.

MY APHRODISIAC

The more I am with you, the more I need you,
Whenever, wherever and however
You're my addiction,
Like a forbidden fruit in the Garden of Eden
You are so appealing and irresistible
My passion consumes and it's very hard to restrain
Your temptation just feel so right I can't resist you.
Like a junky on crack cocaine
My one desire craving is you
You got me feeling high as a May cloud
Your elegance, aristocracy and statuesque has transcends
All tangible boundaries of lust.
Mesmerize and entangle, like a prey trapped in a spiderweb
There is just no escaping you
This insatiable feeling is unstoppable
I knowingly and willingly falls for all your lures
Like a victim under a witch magical spell
That you weep oh so well
The way you control me
My body aches with hunger for you
Just one look at you and I become hypnotize
You're my aphrodisiac
I'm so enamored by you
The way your every nuance drive me crazy
You're the one I have no resistance to-to-to
Like Delilah you find way into my head
Where even Angels fear to trend
You are a true reflection
Of God's greatest weakness to mankind.

REFLECTION

When you look in the mirror
You can only see the reflection of yourself
But if you could see yourself the way I see you
You would know you are the most unfathomable beauty
God have created
No one fortunate enough to realize what a gold mine you are
Not even the highest bidder could claim such priceless possession
To capture such rarity I would have to be a thief
Your magnificence and sparkling beauty dazzle me with glow
Like vivid blue diamonds
You are priceless in every way imaginable
You are such a rarity
The treasure every man wants to own
The princess every king wants to crown
It's amazing one woman having everything from head to toes
It's as if you were handcrafted by a craftsman's chisel
Not even Picasso could paint such a flawless imagery.

LIFE LESSONS

Successful people know that failure
And struggle is a part of being successful
Don't be afraid to take chances
Sometimes things seems impossible until it's done
So embrace the lesson
Learn from your failures
Don't give your doubts too much time
Nor be blinded by what virtue there is
Stay committed to your goals, dreams,
aspirations and decisions
But also flexible in your approach
Be very cautious in your affairs
Take kindly to correction
It will nurture strength of spirit
to shield you in sudden misfortune
Endurance and patience is where
your inner strength lies
Nothing in life is a coincidence
Everything you're experiencing is meant to be
So don't let your fear speak too loud
Believe in yourself
Be humble in your quest to find success
You're braver than you think
more determine and talented than you know
and way more capable than you imagine.

MISSING YOU

The thoughts of you surround me
My love I'm enchanted by you
I can't stop thinking of you
You are driving me crazy
Everything you are, I am not
I will break the rules for you
There are no ways or how,
whether high, low or in-between
There is nothing I wouldn't do for you
You are so special to me
Words cannot express
The indescribable joy and happiness you bring
Making my life nicer than it's ever been
You are the love of my life
My love for you is so special
I will always crave for you
My feelings couldn't be denied
I will always desire you
You have me so completely
I cherish you every second of each day
You are everything to me
You are perfect for my heart
Our love is always transcending
When I'm with you I feel so extraordinary
Each memory of you is fills with sweet emotion
You illuminated my soul with happiness
I give you my deepest devotion
There's nothing I could ever say
And nothing I could do.
To let you know just how much I am in love with you
Even if things seems like they won't work out

I will never give up on you
I will be patient
I will be kind
I will be honest
I will be loyal
I promise to love you unselfishly always
You are the only one who has ever meant this much to me
The way I feel about you
With you, my life is so blessed.

UNAPOLOGETICALLY

I have spoiled too many unworthy people
with love, time and attention
I have made them the center of my universe
And in return they only see me as one of their many options
I'm not comparing myself to no one
Neither am I perfect
But if you are not contributing to my growth and development
You are a distraction
When we allow mediocrity in others in also increases your mediocrity
Some will wish you the best and hate you when you get it
I am embracing my difficult and unique journey called life
I'm only giving my energy to what fulfills me
Everything in life is either an opportunity to grow
or an obstacle to keep you from growing
Don't watch the clock; do what it does keep going forward
Some people come into your life like a dark storming night
When the storm is over and the sun rises it becomes a beautiful day
It washes away the unnecessary.

TRULY YOURS

I love your sweet smile
I love your beautiful brown eyes
I love your adorable dimples
I love your sexy pink lips
I love your chocolate skin
I love your perfectly curves body
I love your gentle hugs
I love your soft touch and the warmth of your embrace
I love that you love me
The way that I am
You makes me feel adored
I love that I love you
The way you are
And need you like no one before and still crave you more and more
I can't find words to describe this feeling inside
It only takes a second to get me from here to there
The happiness I can't hide
This kind of Joy money can't buy
I want our lips to touch and our hands to hold
I want to feel your body comfort me when I am cold
I want to kiss you in public and around your mom and not be afraid
In the morning when I wake up
It's your face I want to see and tell you how much I truly love you.

THOUGHTS

The happiness of your life depends
upon the quality of your thoughts
You are responsible for you own happiness
In fact, you create it
You attract it
You are the architect of your own reality
What you think you become
So be a reflection of what you need in your life
If you need inspiration
Be someone else motivator
If you need sunshine
Be the rainbow in someone else cloud
If you need joy
Be someone else happiness
If you need trust
Be someone else confidant
If you need comfort
Be someone else refuge
If you need love
Be someone else
Companionship
Because no one ever live or leave this world
without someone else's intervention.

WHAT WE HAVE

Our love isn't just anything or something
What we have is beyond comparison
You are the most precious thing I've ever been given
There will never be enough words to describe
just how much I love you
You are not just anyone or someone
You are the most amazing, sweetest,
most caring person I have ever met
You're undoubtedly my heart's greatest delights
Every time I look in your eyes I see it
My present and my future
You are in my dreams at night
and my thoughts throughout the day
I never thought I could love someone in every single way.

THINKING OF YOU

My mind is always on you
I taught of you yesterday and the day before that too.
A matter of fact I am thinking of you right now
I think I might be losing my mind
So happily excited
Thinking about you is the next best thing to being with you
Reminiscing on all the things we'll do and all the places
we'll go when your here with me
You mean the universe to me and no matter what I write for you,
It is absolutely impossible to explain what I have in my heart for you.
My soul feels connected to you every single day of my life.
Today even while I am writing this
I am falling in love with you all over again
deeper and deeper each passing seconds.
My heart skips a beat every second, every moment I am not with you
Completely in love and terrified
Afraid of losing you
Makes me go crazy
Makes me go mad
Makes me sad
Yet my heart is overwhelm with happiness
Still can't believe you're actually mine
I don't know what magic that makes people as wonderful as you
But how incredible thankful I'm to have you as my wife.

PERCEPTION

The reality is, you could be amazing, genuine, and sincere,
and still be taken for granted
Some people will only respect you as much as they can use you
Never be anyone's toilet paper
Where you're either on a disposable roll
Or taking shit from someone else
You're the architect of your own portrait
What you paint
Will ultimately determine how people sees you
Like the rainbow let your true colors stands out in any cloud
You are the artistry of you own masterpiece
When you allow others to paint
Your reality
You will only be a copy version of yourself
So don't allow anyone to dull your shine
Just like moons and just like suns
With certainty of tides
You will never fulfill your true potential
Until you find your true purpose in life.

BROKEN

I lie here all alone sad and broken
Why do I care to love or die?
Unable to sleep
My heart wounded stabbed with a knife and I am left to die.
You say I was your blue sky but you turn mine into rain.
My broken heart and shedding tears
Has become the topic of the day online
You said you love me and keep telling me
How much you care but you never really did.
The way you tore my heart and drained my soul
I live every day in pain
Everything in my world has turn to gray
I gave you all my love and in return you gave me hurt
We use to be something now we are nothing
What started out so sweet and reassuring.
Ended painfully in disrespect, lies, deceit and fights
Will this pain ever go away?
As the evening sun sets the harsh reality creeps in
One more night of crying myself to sleep…

Some say I'm Black and beautiful
Some say I'm white and beautiful
Others say beauty is in the eyes of the beholder
But the true essence of beauty doesn't define by the color of our skin.

LIFE'S STRUGGLES

Some say it's too hard living
Others say hard work is the key to success
But neither sum up the real struggles of life
Some of us live from paycheck to paycheck
Others are living below the poverty line
While some are dying from hunger
Never has poor people struggles more foreseen
Never has the cry for help trumpet louder
Struggling with challenges that continuously reappear
Constantly battling the iniquities of life
Only leave us submersed in despair
Fearful of what lies ahead and equally fearful of turning back
Along way down on every side
What tranquil serenity?
Like the rich and powerful in Cherry Gardens
But the harsh reality of life's struggles in Tivoli Gardens.

LIFE'S ASPIRATIONS

Some say to be poor is a crime but to be rich and
famous comes with a price just as much.
You may not be rich and famous like Bill Gates,
But you can still achieve your own wealth and fame.
You may not be as inspiring and articulate as
the great Martin Luther King Jr.,
But you can still get your points across.
You may not be as talented and gifted like Picasso is with art,
But we individually possess our own unique gifts and talents.
You may not have the will power, determination
and strength like Nelson Mandela
to rise to the top after years of injustice and hardship,
But we all have been through trials and tribulations at some point
or another in our lives and overcome like gladiators.
You may not be as smart and brilliant as Steve Jobs
who stunned the world and created Apple,
But we as individuals can create our own impact on society.
You may not be as innovative as the creator of space
shuttle to travel through space and time,
But the inventor of the kitchen fork is just
as brilliant they are being used
by millions around the globe every day.
You may not be as fast Usain Bolt who stunned the
world by running 9.58 seconds in a 100m race,
But we can all cross the finish line regardless of our position.
We only fail when we stop in our tracks.

Eyes have never seen
Minds have never dreamt
Thoughts have never conjured up
Books try to explain
Movies try to portray
Novelties dress it up
Documentaries mess it up
Scientist struggle to find a cure
Hospital full to capacity
Morgues full to capacity with dead bodies
Never has such tranquil serenity
Ends in bitter, sweet
Mass plantation of lost souls on secret fields
The most unprecedented smell of flesh and blood
leaping in bitter air
What planes?
What ships?
What Superior?
What King and rulers of world?
What signs of normalcy?
But just panic and desperation
Never has poor people struggled more forscene
What bliss?
The world is at a standstill
Bird's tweets interrupted
Wild animals walk the street freely
As dawn blinks, its appearance,
The sky nod to him
Who is King?
Trees bow their heads in awe! In anticipation of nightfall
Stars remind us how magnificent they are.
The desert rejoice rain at last
The Earth fights back
As crows fly overhead looking for a meal
A brief effusion of Rosy smoke as the planet sings
A breath of fresh air
Before its regular transparency resumed.

MY JAMAICAN QUEEN

Girl, I love you like a Jamaican mango
You are to me like ackee and saltfish
My national dish
Your lips so sweet
Like something glazed with raspberry nectar
You astound me
Like our national flag
Black, green and gold
Skin of chocolate and heart of gold
And perennial as the grass
You are stunning and beautiful
As Dunn's river falls
Your skin soft like coco butter
And rich as blue mountain coffee beans
You are mystical as black river
Such a pleasure to behold
You are breathtaking
Like Negril's seven miles of white sand beaches
You dazzle me like a Kingston City's sunset's bright orange glow
You are intoxicating like Appleton run
Distinction, flavored with delight, smooth as lustful
You are irresistible as a cold Red Stripe Beer
On a Jamaican hot summer day
You have more curves than Firm Gully
You are the archetype of gorgeousness
In every inch, perfection is sustained
Your beauty inspires freedom songs and poems
I will fight for you like Nanny and the maroons
You are a supreme being, supreme creation, the Queen of Jamaica.
Such a beautiful sight
Angels congregate around you, so that they can reflect you glory
You are a goddess.

I still believe in chasing dreams
Like my ancestors
I'm hungry still
To see what's down road beyond the hills
The people in your life will either have
a positive or negative impact on you
Some will only be there for you as much as they can use you
So surround yourself with people who push you,
motivates you, believes in you
Who challenges you to be your best
Their strength will allow you to hurdle through life's challenges
When you have the right persons in your life
you channel their energy into greatness
You never really know the true impact you have on those around you
So always be a positive influence
Inspire and empower those around you
Let wisdom guide you through the best course on life's journey
Because no one ever live or leaves this world
without someone else's intervention
So if those around you are not contributing
to your growth and development
They are not your people.

You know why I am always happy?
Because I'm an optimist
I know that success is a journey not a destination
It's not always about greatness but consistency
The only difference between ordinary people
and extraordinary people
Is that ordinary people are wishers
And extraordinary people are doers
Excellence is not an act, but a habit
The world is not static, it's in motion
Success seems to be connected with action
So if you stay one place too long
Success will pass you by
Either you run with enthusiasm, determination,
strength, and courage
Or failure, disappointment, hardship,
and struggles will run you over.

Sometimes in life it's unappreciated
And ungrateful persons in your circles
Why you are struggling
You would be amazed if you let them go
The tremendous blessings that comes your way.

The limitations of writing your own story
The challenges of tracing your dreams and aspirations
The road to success is full of obstacles
It's almost impossible to complete your journey
without someone else's intervention
Individual talent may win games,
But team work and intelligence win championships
Life is like a 4x4 relay where it takes team work to be victorious
You have to rely on each individual effort and commitment
It is the fuel that allows unknown people
to attain unprecedented results
Nothing is more common than unsuccessful people with talent
But never fulfill their true potential and purpose in life
Because they can never see beyond themselves
Teamwork makes the dream work
Individualism will never take you anywhere
No world renowned invention was created
by only one person effort and input
A genius will not; unrewarded another genius
For his or her brilliance and expertise
The more brilliant minds
The easier problems get solved and solution found
The optimist sees opportunity in every difficulty
One of the biggest differences between
Being successful and unsuccessful is
Too few of us are doers, while too many of us are wishers.

A FOOL'S GOLD

The price of love is sometimes life itself
The unforgiven crimes of loving someone too much
Either I'm stupid, I'm foolish, or you're playing me
It's strange how I invested so much into something
that will never make me a profit
It strange I keep holding on to something I cannot change
It's rather strange my arms long for something it cannot hold
She is the love of my life and I was destined to love her
I'm not the love of her life and she's destined not to love me
But it's strange I love something that I cannot have
It's totally strange my heart aches for something I will never have
Unrealistic I am making plans for the future
for something I don't even have in reality
Definitely strange I'd hope for something that will never come.

Success is a formula
If not carefully formulated with the right ingredients
You will never accomplish your goals, dreams and aspirations
There will always be doubters, as well as critics and nonbelievers
It's the mindset, drive, determination, strength, will power
and self-belief that one has that nothing is insurmountable
Every huddle can be move if you push
That will ultimately determine how successful you become in life
Success isn't define by how one's accumulated his or her wealth
Weather good or bad
Success is success and it's not judgmental
A coward will tell you it can't be done
But an optimist see opportunity in every difficult situation
The greater the difficulty, the more enthusiasm in surmounting it
Success don't just happen, you create it
Don't let the fear of losing be greater than the joy of winning
Neither give your doubts too much time
The attitude you bring, the determination you have
and the goals you set will result
in the level of success you accomplish
Don't let someone else's opinion of you become your reality
So much so that it overshadowed your dreams
Never miss out on the opportunity to become
a better version of yourself every day.

When you give too much importance to people
They think you're always free
They fail to realize
You make yourself available for them every time
They take your kindness for weakness
They see your awareness as ignorance
They take your silence for speechless
They take your love for granted
They deceived and mistreats you
But we are discovering that, there are people in our lives
who can never be please
Don't allow yourself to be manipulated and use by others
Self-control is strength
Don't allow your emotions to overpower your intelligence
Don't let others define you and don't let your past confine you
You are responsible for your happiness
In fact, you create it
You attract it
You manifest it
You have to realize there are certain things in life you cannot control
and the heart of another person is one them
It's time to put aside people who don't see your true worth
When you beginning to understand the value of your worth
You will realize there are some situations that no longer deserve
Your time, dedication, energy, and focus
You need to walk away from the practice of pleasing people
who choose to never see your value
And from any thought that undermines your peace of mind
The more you disassociate yourself from things that poison your soul,
the happier your life will be.

Keep your mind focus
Keep your dreams alive
Keep your eyes on the prizes
Keep your heart open
Trust your spirit and believe in yourself
The happiness of your life depends on the quality of your thoughts
The quality of your life depends on the vision of your mind
The quality of your success depends on the
strength of your determination
And the direction of your life depends on the level of your focus
The goals in life worth achieving require dedication,
time, planning, effort and persistence
You are the architect of your reality
In fact, you create it
You are responsible for how people view you
Anything you do or say gets filtered through the lens of others
So always be mindful of your actions
There will always be doubters, as well as critics and nonbelievers
Don't let others opinion confined you
Always rise above their criticism
You are not define by your charisma but by your character
Always live with the consciousness that others will be affected
if you fail or fall.

PARADISE PLUM

People say one woman can't have everything
Some say beauty is in the eyes of the beholder
Others say God made all women equal
But every time I look at you
I realize God must have spent a lot more time on you
To create someone so perfect
Like the reflection of his heart
Not a single blemish have I seen in your frame
From your hair follicles to your toenails
Perfection is sustained
Even the most beautiful Angels in heaven pour rain
To see such flawless beauty here on earth
Even scientist can't explain your remarkable beauty
You are the geographically wonders of science
You test every limits of humanity
The glow of your beauty radiates like diamonds
Whenever you smile the whole world is astonished
You cuteness knows no bounds
Your sexiness has no limits
Your adorableness has no imperfections
The way you walk like you're on Broadway
Commands every man's attention
You are truly one of a kind
The most stunning being in the universe.

If I was a billionaire for my fortune I wouldn't care
Because I love you like my savings
You are a priceless treasure that money can't buy
Like the stock exchange
You are everything I want to invest in
You are rare as fancy red diamonds
Africa's most beautiful
You are sweet like a gardenia flower
You are more beautiful than Bella Hadid
You are such an unframed masterpiece
You are stunning and magical like an eclipse
Your skin smooth like molasses and beautiful
Like melted chocolate
You are more gorgeous than the
Seven wonders of the world combined
Like a morning mist you are such a pleasure to behold
In all your splendor
The sexiness you display
Have men swam around you like a hive of honey bees
You are by far the most beautiful woman to ever grace this earth
A goddess is what you are.

When positivity becomes the core of your thinking
and determination your driving force
You rise to the occasion
You see the invincible
Feel the intangible, achieve the impossible
and overcome the insurmountable.

Nothing in life is ever given
If you need something you will find a reason
If you are afraid you will find excuses
You are responsible for you own destiny
The sooner you realize that
The better equip you will be to handle life's challenges
So many of us live from day to day without a real sense of purpose
Constantly blaming others for our mistakes
and the decisions we make
We refuse to take responsibility for our own lack of achievement
Instead we focus on goals that are all about proving ourselves
Rather than developing and acquiring new skills
Everyone journey is different
Believing in your ability to succeed is key
Unapologetically, you are responsible for the path you choose travel
You are responsible for you own journey
You have to realize that there are consequences
to every decision you make in life
So make the best of your opportunity when it comes
People will make plans and set goals when the sun is shining
And make excuses when the storm comes
Either learn to walk between the rain drops or prepare
to deal with the mud
And that's the roughest part about being on a journey
You have to learn to embrace adversity
Never underestimate the difficulties of reaching your goals
Creating and sustaining your motivation is instrumental
Never settle for average
Always bring your best to the moment
Determination is the anchor between success and failure
And discipline is the bridge between goals and accomplishment
Never give up on your passion
Because passion bring progress
And progress brings consistency.

THE BLUEPRINT

We are divine creations of our creator
We are the blueprint of evolution
In fact the earth was once black
Before God created light
Even space is dominated by the color black
Yet your skin color give you the audacity
To think somehow you are superior to us
Black people have been under attack
For many centuries, it's time to react
We are fed up, we're tired of being oppressed
Even though our ancestors have fought for freedom,
injustice, racism and equal rights
Today the battle still rage on
They define everything by the color of our skin
They call us Black American, Black Chinese,
Black Indians, and Black African
Everything Black
Even our history they call it Black
They envy our strength, yet minimize our potential
But hold your head high
You are pointing to the stars with pride
They see our awareness as ignorance
But we are discovering that justice is blindfold
with its head bowed
They see freedom of speech as feminist
When we stand with humility and in solidarity
They try to divide us with their individualism doctrine
They consider our sassiness, swag and uniqueness strange
They call our languages slangs
They consider our success accidental
Any recognition is preferential treatment

To voice our concerns is discontentment
They see our courage as challenge to their cynicism
If we don't believe them, they see us as adversaries
They see our observation and bravery as potential
Threat
They take our kindness for weakness
They take our silence for unawareness
They see equality as surrendering to minority
The color of our skin makes us victims
They are constantly looking for ways to rewrite our history
With their bitter twisted lies.

PARADISE PLUM

If there was an award for the best girlfriend ever
I'm sure you would have won
If there was a prize for beauty
I'm sure you would have won for being the most beautiful!
If there was a gift for being the sweetest,
I'm sure you would have gotten the most expensive one of all
Because you are the sweetest thing God has ever created
It's like he glazed you with nectar
If there was a trophy for being the cutest
I'm sure you would have a room full
Because your adorableness has no flaws,
no faults nor imperfections
I will go as far as to say
You are a goddess
If there were prize money for the best qualities
I'm sure you would be a billionaire
Because everything that you are and possess
sings nothing but pure perfection
Your listless qualities and attributes are comparable
to that of an angel so divine
If there was a medal for sexiness
I'm sure you would have won all gold
Not a single blemish have I seen in your portrait
If there was an honor for being the most amazing person
I'm sure you would have top the Queen's high achievers
If there was an auction not even a billionaire's fortune
could claim such unframed masterpiece
You are priceless in every way.

Young Black men rise to the occasion
You have been under attack
For many centuries, it's time to react
Take a stride and claim your place in society
You were born with the heart of a thousand fathers
Men without limits
Men without boundaries
Slave of the cane fields
Soldiers for justice to gladiator on the battlefield
Your forefathers were dehumanized, oppressed,
denigrated, stereotyped and mistreated
Yet in spite of the shackles they rose over the hills
to see the light, to see freedom
Young Black men
Represent your Black race, your roots, and your culture
Let them be aware that all Black men are great
Hold your head high you are pointing to the stars with pride
Standing tall on the backs of your ancestor's achievements
With so much emphasis placed on the word "Black men"
Your black skin tells a story
It's not just a color
But a symbol of bravery
It's a form of expression
It's a medal of freedom
An award of resilience
Your very existence is essential
Black man whose fore-parents were once slaves
Young Black men it's your time to shine
Never be afraid to be seen
There is power in your youth and strength
in your diversity

Let us all unite
And stand in humility and solidarity
Young men of African descent
You are so much more than little Black boys
who grew up in poverty
A success story of a nation
Like Barack Obama
From poverty, raise by a single parent
To the president of the most powerful and successful
nation on earth
A role model and aspiration to all Black man
The recognition of a true success story
The Apennine of a great Black man
From nothing to the highest of the heights.

How you see yourself will ultimately shape
Your life
Your success
Your character
Your vision
Your mindset
Your determination
Your values
Your opinion
Your belief
Your passion
So be a reflection of greatness
Believing in your ability
To succeed is enormously important
In achieving your goals
Not fearing the unfamiliar
Life is full of situations
That are not always clear
Perseverance and willpower will guide you
Through the challenges that lies ahead
So take control of your priorities
Focus and pursue goals that is achievable
Don't let the fear of failure be greater than the joy of success
Greatness comes from taking actions
When you are intrinsically motivated, nothing is impossible
Every new challenge is met
Don't allow negativity frequent your head space
When positivity becomes the core of your thinking
You see the invincible,
Feel the intangible,
Achieve the impossible and overcome the insurmountable.

PARADISE PLUM

The only woman I ever truly love
This type of love I can't explain
The type I cannot compare
The type that money can't buy
The type that cannot be quantified
The type that cannot be characterize
It's like heaven frozen in time
Every day with you is a wonderful surprise
Especially different every time
My soul raises when we collide
I realize this love I feel will never subside
We are divinely entwine
The chemistry we share is unparalleled
Too hard to fake it, nothing can replace it
Even God with his righteous eyes looking from up high
Realize this love can never be denied
She is truly divine
Her eyes sparkle diamonds
Her cheeks glow like candle in the night
Her smile is captured by a thousand satellites
Her body sings trap queen
In every inch perfection is sustained
Admirable like the rainbow
You crave to have it
Crave to touch it
You watch it with great awe!
Like beautiful art
So many things so different about her
Because so many things so right about her
Her sexiness is always on display
Such blissful looks of affection

Gives me a feeling from the tips of my testicles
All the way up to my spine
As I sway from side to side
Feeling so high
I realize this love I feel for you will never die
You make all my senses smile
Got me feeling so hypnotize
By the essence that's wonderfully you
She makes my heart beat
In a now-now time signature
Like rhythm and rhyme
Synchronized and mesmerize
Every melody is harmonize
The way she makes my heart sings
Like an April breeze on the wings of spring
I never felt like this
So deeply, madly and crazy in love
I'm connected to her completely, mentally, spiritually
And at the same time incredible attracted to her physically
Like the new moon, like diamond in the mines
You dazzle, you sparkle, you glow, and you shine
You are more beautiful than Aphrodite and Cleopatra
The world is astonished by your beauty
Your whole being is phenomenal
There is nothing I would cherish more
In life than making you my Queen.

EVERYTHING BLACK

They call you Black Power, Black Queen,
Black Skin, Black Hair, Black Eyes,
Black Bitches, and Black Witches
They hate your skin color
They try to minimize your confidence and intelligence
You are constantly being scrutinized, stereotyped and judged
Scared of your own image, your own reflection
When you look in the mirror all you sees is imperfection
Bleaching your skin
As if your chocolate skin isn't beautiful enough
Straightening your Afro cause blonde hair ain't tough
Beautiful women of color
Do you ever stop and think
How phenomenal you are?
Defying all expectations and beyond all definition
You were born with the heart of a thousand mothers
Woman without limits, without boundaries
You are a true woman of substance
You are the reign of earth and the creators of life
In fact you are the evolution of light
The glow of your black skin reflects the sunshine
You never have to worry about being pasty or getting a tan
Mother Africa kissed your skin like wind,
infused it with melanin to allow you
to dance with the sun
Beautiful women of color
You are a flower flourishing
through all the criticism, cynicism,
racism and doubtism.
Black girls, you are spectacular, luminous,
A rare black diamond

Whether imitated, exploited, or denigrated
My Black queen
Do you know you are astonishing?
I envy your determination
I salute your courage
I commend your confidence
Your very existence is essential
Black woman whose fore-parents were once slaves
Represent
Your blackness
Your boldness
Your womanliness
The plumpness of your breast
Roundness of your ass
To the stride of your gait, to the span of your arms,
To the depth of your bosom, to the curve of your hips
You are magical
Everywhere you go
From head to toe
Like a Queen Bee
You are immaculately beautiful.

AFRICAN PRIDE

Women of African descent
Your beauty has not gone unseen
Your talents has not gone undiscovered
Your strength, confidence, courage, and boldness
has not gone unrecognized
Your resilience has not gone unnoticed
You have been stereotyped, mistreated
and dehumanize by others
But you are celebrated by your people
Black excellence, the recognition and empowerment of our people
Black woman you are a Queen
Your skin is beautiful like melted chocolate and rich as molasses
Nothing compared to your glorious shades of melanin
Weather dark, light or mix racial
Your ebony skin allows you to glisten in the sun
and glow in the moonlight
Your beauty cannot be imitated or diluted
Let them and beware that all Black woman are flawless
You were born with an immeasurable soul
In spite of shackles our ancestors rose over the hill
to see our future, to see the light,
to see freedom
With so much emphasis on the word "Black"
Your skin tells a story
It's not only a color
But a symbol of bravery
It's a mountain of courage
It's more than just race
It's a form of expression
It's a museum of strength
It's pride for your heritage, tradition, roots and culture

It's a lifestyle you must live
Your black skin is a badge of superiority
More than just the word "majestic"
It's a medal of freedom
An award of confidence
Black woman
You are a flower; you can grow anywhere
You are strong
You are resilient
You are beautiful
Proudly proclaiming what makes you unique
Black, beautiful and proud.

MONEY

The root of all evil
The tree of greed
The branches of jealousy
The blossom of envy
The fruit of distastefulness
When we are motivated
By jealously and greed, or both
It consumes us
It takes first place in our lives other than our creator
It becomes a slave master in our lives
It motivates and drive us to lie, steal, cheat,
gamble, embezzle, and even murder
Money, the red eye
The more we accumulate, the more we crave
People who are obsessed with money
Lack the godliness and contentment in God's eyes
And the sad thing is that
In the interval between life and death
We are here constantly fighting for what we did not bring
And for what we will not take with us.

Life is the reflection and accumulation of the choices we make
No opportunity is given if you need something you have take it
If you really want to be successful
You will find a way if you don't you will make excuses
Successful people always have a purpose to fulfil and goals to achieve
They always begin with the end in mind
If you know where you are going any road will take you there
Sometimes being successful is not always about what you achieve
But what you have overcome on your journey
A passionate person knows that very few
things comes with a guarantee
It's the way you think, it's the way you create
It's your belief, it's your passion, and it's your determination
It's your principles and attitude
Anyone can have a brilliant idea but it's what you do with it
that will makes the difference
You will never be successful without the right mindset
An explorer see opportunity in every wrong turn
They know it will take them to a new destination
You have to learn to take risk
Sometimes things seems impossible until it's done
Every new discovery was discovered by someone
who was willing to push boundaries.

When you look in the mirror
You can only see the reflection of outer selves
A reflection of your portrait doesn't define you
What really matters is not your reflection but your character
Don't let others image of you undermine or confine you
Never limit yourself because of others limited imagination
Perception is in the eyes of the beholder
There is no limits to what you can accomplished
You truly hold the master key to the world you live
A judgmentalist will always perceive you to be
Whatever they need you to be
So surround yourself with people who truly see your best self
Your limitations is only your imagination
Believing in yourself is key
Greatness comes from within
You are the architect of your own destiny
In the end what will matter is not your level of success
But your significance
Your contribution to others growth, dreams and aspirations.

Live life in the moment
Tomorrow was not promised and neither is today
The greatest joy in life is the present
So live it to the fullest like you will die tomorrow.

You are the only limitation of yourself
You can steer yourself in any direction you choose
Any path you choose will eventually take you to a destination.

The greatest revenge in life is success
The greatest come back is progress
The greatest joy is consistency
And the greatest satisfaction in living is contentment.

The true essence of time is the most precious thing given
If you don't keep track of it you might end up wasting it
Never wait for a next day arrive nor let
yesterday use up too much of today
Tomorrow isn't promise and neither is today
So make the best of every moment.

Accept no one's definition of your life
You are the artist of your own reality
What you paint will ultimately define you
Believing in yourself is instrumental in how
you transform your defeat into victory
Clear your mind of self doubt
You will never achieve your goals doubting yourself
Don't let yesterday failure be a hindrance of today's success
Memory lane is for people who gave up on their dreams
Be proud of yourself
Follow your dreams
Exceed your passion
Maximize your potential
Capitalize on your strength
Minimize your weakness
Don't let your past confine you
Every situation in life is temporary
See obstacles and challenges as learning experience
and not as failure
Every success story is not by chance but by choice.

ALONE

Lying thinking late last night
How to find my soul mate
Where lover's intuition lies
Thirsty for a sip of affection
My deep yarning unnourished
My immense hunger unfulfilled
Unable to sleep
Fate or destiny, call it what you want
But nobody knows.

YOU

You are earth's finest creation
You are an angel in disguise
You are amazingly, undoubtedly,
unquestionable
My heart greatest delight
You woo me
You groove me
You soothe me
You enchant me
You ignite me
You entice me
You excite me
You co-write me
You school me
Ain't nobody like you.

Love arrives and in its train come ecstasies
It was like a ticking time bomb
It's rather strange how it happened
It came
It went
It never lasted for long
It just happened
I guess it was supposed to happen that way
I had my share
And even though I'm satisfied
I'm hungry still
I guess it was never meant to be
It was a lesson that should have been taught
A lesson that should have been learned
It had an ultimatum
And I guess that much it conveyed
I'm not stuck on wondering why it did
When it did
It came
It went
It happened
It took the very heart of me with it
I barely understood it
Like a predator stalking its prey
It knows my weaknesses
It took a piece of me
That seemed desperate to find love
It came
It went
It happened
It went without apology
I enjoy it when it came
For a brief moment
I enjoyed it while it lasted
But the moment it went I knew
When only the smell of your love

lingers in my silk sheets
Only then, I can greedily consume your presence.

Good-looking men wonder where my confidence lies
I'm not cute or wear designer clothes
Nor built to suit a male fashion model's size
I say,
"It's the swag in my step
The confident in my style
It's in the strength of my shoulders
The size of my shoes
It's the level of my intelligence
It's the level of my boldness
It's the level of my success
It's the color of my skin
It's the proudness of my race
I'm a man
Out of many one people
I will never be afraid to be seen
The Apennine of a great man
That's me"

WITHOUT DADDY'S CARE

It's true every beautiful gifts comes from heaven
It's also true, Mom, you are the giver of life
First, it was the warmth of your protective womb
Then your arms were molded into a smart crib, to rock me to sleep
Also the nourishment of your breast milk spur me into growth
The freshness and softness of your bosom were my comfort
And the air I breathe the essence that's wonderfully you, Mom
It's also true if there was an award for the best mom
I'm sure you would have won
When God gave me to you
That's the best thing he could ever do.

Mother,
You're raised a child with flair
During those early days without Daddy's care
You gave me confident, looks and brain
I was too young to understand your struggles and daily sacrifice
Among all your other concerns
Now I understand you had a larger plan in life for me
Even without Daddy's care
You were my mentor and guide
I'm sure you are aware
You were bless with an amazing golden child.

The importance of thinking things through for yourself
You are what you believe yourself to be
Always think highly of yourself
Be proud of who you are
Don't let others limited imagination of you
makes you feel differently
Every day is another chance
to be a better version of your self
Trust your intuition
Surround yourself with positive people
Learn to distance yourself from all negativity
Believing in yourself is the most powerful self-assurance
Self-confidence and self-worth
Embrace your skill and talents
It will enable you to find your true passion
Life is about choices
Follow your dreams
Stop comparing yourself to others
Everyone journey is different
Accomplishments drive ambition
Determination fuel success
And persistence bring consistency.

A poor man's reality

Your life I can only live in my imagination
My life you cannot even see it in your imagination.

The integrity of a great woman
Mrs. Michelle Obama
You are a magical wonder
Voice of a nation, First Lady, Role model, Advocate
Whatever the title is, it echoes across
the length and breadth
of America, the Caribbean, all the way to Africa
A strong Black woman beyond all definition
Do you know you are astonishing?
I envy your strength
I salute your courage
I commend your confidence
Young American girls congregate around you
that they can reflect your courageousness,
determination and vision
You are everything they wants to emulate
You are the topic of discussion
In every school
You are a museum of treasure
America can never replace
A symbol of eloquent
You are definitely a credit to your race
First Lady of the most powerful nation on earth
to the Mothers of Africa
Weather celebrated, exploited, or denigrated
Like suns, like moons and like the safari dust
With certainty of tides
You shine, you glow, and you rise
My Black queen
You are pointing to the stars with pride
You are not intimidated by anyone or anything
Inspiration for the future
You are so much more than the little Black girl
who grew up in poverty on the south side of Chicago
The success story of a country
A vision for yourself and for your people

Your numerous accolades cemented your place in history
You graduated from Princeton University
You also studied at Harvard Law School
You didn't stop there
You are also the vice president for the
community and external affairs
of the University of Chicago Medical Center
You exceeded all expectations
You are honorable, patient and focused
and flexible, determine and dynamic
You speak, with boldness and purpose
A Black woman whose fore-parents were once a slaves
You are America's crowning achievement
The recognition of a great Black woman
Who have done it all?
Michelle Obama,
You makes us all proud
Your credentials stretch wide and far
You deserve all distinction there is
A strong Black woman on a mission.

The book of life has many pages and chapters
What your write will ultimately determine
how successful your story is
Make your story the best one to ever written,
a bestseller fill
With adventures to tell, lesson to learn
and good deeds to remember
Always live your best, do your best and think your best
The possibilities are endless
Life is always evolving and transforming
Even though your story is being written by you
You will never know what the next chapter holds
Because the validity of life's breathe can be
cancelled at any time
Tomorrow was never promise and neither is today
And that's sad thing about life's journey—
In the interval between life and death,
you don't hold the master key
So make the best of every moment
Live it to the fullest because there was but is no yesterday
and there maybe to tomorrow.

Life is no straight and easy corridor
It's full of uncertainty
But your determination and inner strength will not only show
in your ability to persist but also your ability
to overcome adversity
Don't judge each day by what you have accomplished
but by what you have overcome
Determination will ultimately bring satisfaction
Life itself has no limitations, except the ones you make
It's a challenge, meet it
It's a dream, realize it
It's a journey, complete it
Never stop believing in yourself
Excellence is not an act, but a habit
There is no success without setbacks
You have to be willing to take risk
Even when it seems insurmountable
Your struggles will eventually bring progress
If you have no expectations of yourself you have already failed
When you're are motivated and driven for greatness
You care less about how your life looks to others
but how you feel about yourself
Passion and courage doesn't always roar sometimes
It's the calmness of your thoughts that moves mountains
You will never be successful without the right mindset and attitude.

I think you are the most beautiful thing God
have created, second to life itself
I look at you and I'm so carried away by your remarkable beauty
From your hair follicles all the way down to your toenails
Truly wondrous and completely amazing
one woman having everything
Indescribable by words
You would be my definition of perfection
Your outer finesse has no flaws, no faults nor imperfections
I think your whole being is beautiful
Your gracefulness completely takes my breath away
Your sunbeam liked smile mesmerize
Your ebony eyes magnetized
Your birthing hips and indulging thighs hypnotized
Your vanilla flavored lips are like a scarlet
ribbon such a temptation to kiss
You are such a remarkable magnanimous
reflection of poignant empathy.

Deal with yourself as an individual worthy of respect
And make everyone deal with you the same way
Your self-worth is determined by you
Don't allow others to use you or intimate you
Value yourself and know your worth
Learn to care less about what others think of you
And care more about what you think of yourself
Your value doesn't decrease based on someone's inability
To see your true worth
Be proud of who you are
Always set boundaries
The more you challenge yourself the higher your expectations become
Believing in yourself is one of life's greatest accomplishment
Don't let others limited perception define you
You should always have a clear vision of
what you want to become in life
And pursue your goals, dreams and aspirations
The more confidence you have
The more passionate and enthusiastic you are about life.

Stop letting people tell you
That you can be anything you want to be in life
They are never further from the truth
Because you can never cheat your destiny
Your circumstances reflects your reality
And will ultimately determine how successful you become in life
You can't tell a blind person to see the future
Nor a deaf person to listen
You will never see a rat and a cat go to the same school
But both can accomplish their goals
In the end we are who we are
You can never tell a follower to lead
You will never see the sun fall rain
Everything has its purpose
And so do you
A slave priority is to survive
Not fancy dreams and endlessly possibilities
So embrace your own journey and your accomplishments
whether great or small
You only fail if you quit trying
You don't have to be the inventor of airplanes
to travel through space, time and continents
But the inventor of cars is just as brilliant
They are used by millions around the globe
to compute every day.

You may try to rewrite my history
With your hatefulness and bitter twisted lies
You may try to stifle my growth
But like oceans I spread far and wide
You may minimize my opportunity to potential
But like mountains I stand tall
You may silence my voice
But like the wind my presence is still felt
Even in a crowd I still stand out
You may try to dull my shine
But like suns, like new moons,
Like diamonds in mines
I shine bright, I sparkle, I dazzle, and I glow
You may try to keep me down
But like an eagle I will soar high
Pride for my race makes me a victim
My character is constantly under attack
Being scrutinized, stereotyped, mistreated and misjudged
Men themselves have wondered
Why I haven't buckled, hang my head down and cry
I say, it's the fire in my spirit
The Joy in my feet
The stride of my steps
The reach of my arms
The power in my resilience
The confidence in my style
The strength of my courage
And the immeasurable soul of my DNA
I was born with the heart of a thousand mothers
Woman without limits, without boundaries
I'm not intimated by anything or anyone
With so much emphasis on the color of my "Black Skin"
I am the representation of my race
My Black Skin is a badge of superiority
Let them be aware that all Black woman are flawless
Indeed I'm a Black Queen

I will never be afraid to be seen
I am the Apennine of a great Black woman
Even when the odds are against me
I survive
I will strive
I will overcome
I will be victorious.

The validity of life is full of ups and downs
My opportunities maybe nonexistent
But my dreams are priceless
People who want you to stay ordinary will tell you
Not to have high expectations or big dreams
But my talents are superior
My aspirations are limitless
My vision is boundless
When people can't put you in a box
They can't minimize your growth or potential
Some people will only see you as their shoes
You are constantly being walk on
They will preach equal opportunities, dignity and respect
But behind close door
Individualism doctrine has never been more foreseen
When we allow mediocrity from others
It will only increase mediocrity in us
When people can't dull your shine
They make excuses about your boldness
When they can't overpower your intelligence
They complain about how you are hard to work with
Don't let others impression of you overshadowed your confidence.

ALONE OUT IN THE COLD

No shining armored to protect me
No distant relatives to save me
I am all alone out here
Everybody busy going about their business
No act of kindness
I sit wondering where I'm gonna turn
A society stained with cruelty
A bitter cold of darkness
Trembling in agony
Got to make it out here all alone
Mountains of despair
But I keep marching on
Courage strikes away the sound of fear
A whisper of faith
Faintly fades travelling through distant clouds
Battered and bruise by the cold winters' storm
Got to make it out here all alone
A jacket of warmth
On the pulse of dawn
Thrilled by its presence
Like hope springing high
Got to make it out here all alone
Trying to change nightmares into dreams of joy
Yes I just got to
I just got to
Make it out here all alone.

Your smile is incomparable
Your touch is insatiable
Your vibe is just incredible
Your beauty is indescribable
You are a heavenly design!!
I am completely stunned by neatness of your perfection.
These are just some of the reasons why my mind go crazy
When I hear the sound of your angelic voice
My hands tremble like earthquake
When I imagine touching your beautiful face
And my ego soars and my heart aches
When I think of your irresistible lips touching mine
I have never felt like this for anyone else but you.

The rich will tell you if you are determined and work hard
you will reach the top
Even when their wealth was inherited
As if you are lazy
And somehow your lack of success
Is a result of you not working hard enough
They constantly minimize your opportunity and potential
Unwilling to promote you even when you are qualify
They only look at the losses of your mistakes
and not see the profits of your achievements
They seem to think when you are dependent
You have no choice but to settle for less
They try to keep your self-esteem low
No encouragement or appreciation for your accomplishments
But we are now discovering that
self-worth, self-confidence, self-awareness,
and self-empowerment is no longer blindfolded
with its head bowed
And equality is no longer handcuffs with its hands behind its back
We are now realizing not only we possess
the ability to play by the rules
but can also make them as well
Defiant hold your head high proudly
proclaiming your uniqueness
Proud of you culture and your heritage
Your identity is your dignity and designation
Confident that you can achieve you're every goal
Regardless of the origin from which you have come
or the color of your skin
It's time for something different
A chance for
Something new
A renewed sense of purpose, a burst of inspiration
It's time for that justification
And this time it's not just an illusion.

BLACK COFFEE

I love my coffee black, no sugar, no milk, and no cream
The darker the beans the more distinct the flavor
Beautiful women of color
Your skin is soft as chocolate sponge cake
And as spotless as crystal-clear blue waters.

You don't need thin lips, straight nose, or blond hair
I love you just the way you are
Black skin, thick hair, big brown eyes, full lips,
round nose, plump breast and wide hips
So naturally beautified.

Beautiful Black girls
Proudly wear your Afro hair or extensions
Be proud of what makes you unique
Your black skin, your features, your confidence,
your culture and your roots.

The glow of your natural beauty cannot be dilute or ignore
You are a Queen never be afraid to be seen
Your perfection deserves all man's attention
There is variety in the color of your skin
and richness in your naturality.

Beautiful Black girls
Study your roots and know you're a goddess
Be a reminder that all Black girls are flawless
Remember that they yearn for your sassiness, swag and rhythm
They want your complexion
Because Mother Africa infused it with a rainbow of melanin.

You are not magic, that's an illusion
You are more than a miracle
An unexpected blessing
Your true identity always stands out even in a crowd
My black coffee beans
Shout it out loud, I am Black, beautiful and proud.

Women of African descent
You were created in the image of perfection
Black queen
Out of many one people and voices of a nation
A true identity to your race
There is power in your resilience and strength in your youth.

I love the color of your skin
Black coffee beans
No tan needed
Because your skin is as beautiful as melted chocolate
My Black Queen
Your whole being is beautiful.

PARADISE PLUM

Every time I see your cute face I just melt away, fall like rain
I simple can't imagine a more beautiful sight
The glow of your beauty shines to the end of the universe
There's such goodness in you
There is a million reasons why I can't love you enough
It's the way your brown eyes sparkle
It's the succulent looks of your pink lips
It's the way your smile shines
It's the way your cuteness dazzle
It's the gracefulness in the way you walk
Like stars gliding across the night sky
It's the warmth and comfort of your hugs
It's how gentle your words are
It's the beauty in everything you do
You are a special being
They say there's no perfect person in the world
Yet from the crown of your head to the soles of your feet
speaks nothing but raw perfection
A virtuous woman is what you are
True beauty only exists in your wonderful presence
I have never met anyone so amazing
You will forever be my Queen
And I vow to love you always
You're everything I hoped for
And everything I prayed for in life.

PARADISE PLUM

Your love is sweet like the nectar of a garden petal
It's warm like the ray of the morning sun
And comforting like a blanket on a cold winter's day
Your love is admirable like the rainbow
It glows like candle in the dark
Your love is magical like a California sunset
Your love is pure like the reflection of God's heart
Like platinum it never rust
Your love is honest and real like a heartbeat
It has its own way of arriving like the season
Always at the right moment
Your love makes all my senses smile for no reason
Like lavas it's not
Apologetic, it just flows without resistance
Your love is life's essentials
It's the pulse in my vain
The thoughts in my brain
It's every breath that I take
It's the dream in my sleep
It's the sparkle of glow in my soul
A love so rare like this will always be with me for keeps
A feeling so sincere
A bond so strong
Build on trust, love, respect and understanding
Our love is always transcending
Sometimes I wonder if it is possible for love to be so amazing
How incredible thankful I am to have you in my life
My princess charming
These feelings for you are alarming!
I'm so in love with you.

My life story is not history
My life story is legendary
I have survive setbacks, challenges,
hunger, poverty, oppression,
injustice and hardship
You may stifle my growth
Minimize my confidence to potential
But my dreams are priceless
My determination and strength is unparalleled
Nothing in life is insurmountable
When you have an unrelenting pursuit for success
A wise man once say, "I have a dream"
But the secret to pursue that dream is to be ready f
or your opportunity when it comes
Optimism is the faith that leads to achievement
So don't let your fear speak too loud
nor give your doubts too much time
Mistakes don't mean you are defeated
An ambitious person knows that failure is a part
of being successful
So they strive with adversity
You don't need their permission to achieve greatness
Because you are standing tall on the backs
of your ancestors' achievements
Defiant, you are pointing towards the stars with pride
The Apennine of a great Black man
Whose fore-parents were once slave
Represent your Black race
Let them be aware that all Black men are great.

You are my sunshine of my life
The warm glow of your love is like the ray of sunshine
That brings a rainbow from the storm
You are undoubtedly, unquestionably my heart's greatest treasure
Everything I'm not
You are.

You makes me laugh
You bring so much Joy to my heart
And meaning to my life
It's beyond comparison
Everything you do
Makes my life worthwhile.

You give me a reason to smile
Even on my worse days
You always have cheer.
It's amazing how every time I need you
At the right moment you are there
Everything you are
I hold dear.

You takes my breath away just being so
Kind, sweet, loving, caring and true
Words simply can't describe
My feelings for you
Everything I cherish
In you I find.

You are a blessing.
The one I cherish and love endlessly
You are an angel
Everything about you is special
You are always appreciated and treasured.

HEAVENLY SENT

You are the true definition of beauty
The elegance of the specimen has been heavenly sent
Like a dahlia flower
You're beyond beauty itself
Your glorious essence cannot be captured
Your sexiness overwhelms me
So sophisticated, modern and divinely engineered
My soul raises when we collide
What a feeling of magnitudinal desire
So hypnotized it cannot be characterized
Around you I feel more twitize
You got me feeling so high
As I sway from side to side
I realize this love I feel will never subside
It exceeds all expectations
Like heaven frozen in time
I look at you and I'm completely lost for words
An insightful and delightful imagery so sublime
It excites both body and mind
Now I see the reason why God created my eyes
It's you
You are radiance
You are brilliance
You are divinity
I never felt this feeling
The way she makes me feel
The way she looks at me
The way I look at her
The way she speak with endless possibilities
of life pleasures galore
She is truly divine

This feeling can never be deny
I am burning inside,
A torch of fire,
This is the type of love I can't explain
The type that money can't buy
The type I have to vocalize
Her soulful eyes mesmerized
Her smile defeats a thousand satellites
Lips so sweet they glazed with nectar
Her voice, smooth like a river flowing in harmony
A girl so fine her gracefulness harmonize
Her beauty I will compare to the daffodils in spring.

THOUGHTS OF YOU

My thoughts of you are like a full moon
shining through a cloudy night sky
My thoughts of you are like raindrops
on a rare dessert rose so beautiful
My thoughts of you are like coffee in the morning
My thoughts of you are like umbrella on a rainy day
It doesn't matter the time or season
You are always on my mind
You gave me hope and inspiration
In the moment of weakness
no matter what wonders my eyes have seen
Nothing in this world compares to the beauty
I see when I look at you
I get short of breath my heart skips a beat
Every time I remember your angelic smile
I had no idea that when we met
I would ever fall so helplessly in love like this
Completely indescribable by words
You showed me love can last an eternity
the way you love me unconditionally
Just makes me want to cry
You never cease to kindle an opalescent happiness
glowing with warmth of cocooning my heart
Wish I could stop time or make my thoughts
and imagination of you last forever.

MY GREATEST TREASURE

You are my motivation
My greatest aspirations
You have capture my heart
My greatest treasure
Loving you
It's my greatest pleasure
It's not very often in this mess-up world
You meet someone so amazing like you
It's truly a blessing to have you in my life
Losing you can never be an option
Like my religion
You're a breath of eternity in a timeless space
You made this once broken guy into a wholesome man
Like so many nights before
Waiting for shooting stars to wish upon
And every time I found one
I wished for someone like you
No one is as special as you are to me
You're the happiness
In my thoughts and the joy in my dreams
Never doubt, baby, that your love is everything
my eyes can see
You're the miracle that makes my life complete
You've made me feel what I haven't felt in awhile
Loved and appreciated
You're my soulmate, my boo bear and my best friend
For you I am thankful to the heavens above
You are the incredulous magical wand; that metamorphoses
With you, my life is fill with love and endless possibilities.

YOUR LOVE

Loving you has made my life so amazing
You bring out the very best in me
You fill my world with laughter
and my nights with beautiful dreams
and feelings that's definitely meant to be
Truly wondrous and completely amazing
having such a remarkable woman in my life
You make every day such a joy to live
I wake up with a smile on my face
Anticipating how you gonna make my day
even more tremendous than the day before
It's you who brightens my universe
like a summer with a thousand Julys
Loving you is so amazing
I sigh! And smile deep within
Thanking the universe for you every day
How is it that whenever I need you,
at the right moment, in just the right way
you draw near?
Never have I missed and appreciate someone so much!
I spend so many moments on my own
trying to be a better man
For you to be happy, I'll do whatever it takes
I look at you and gasp in awe!
Wondering how you're mine
You takes my breath away
and leave me speechless
every time I see you.

MOM

You are my greatest aspirations
My teacher, my comforter, my encourager
My backbone on rough days
My pillar on shaky grounds
My strength on weak days
My guidance on my darkest days
My role model
I look at you
And I see everything I want to emulate
The master of every task
The rarest and brightest gems
Mom, you are such an indescribable blessing
Truly amazing one woman having everything
Sometimes all I can do is smile in awe!
Completely amazed to have such a
Remarkable woman in my life
I love you, Mom.

Happy Mother's Day
From: Son

SHY

I saw you yesterday
And the day before that too
A matter of fact I saw you earlier today
Every time I see you my knees go wobbly
My heart skips a beat and my breath catches in my throat
Completely dumbfounded and lost for words
So captivated, so intimidated by you
You are just too perfect
And way out of my league
By far the most beautiful girl I ever seen
Lost in a maze looking for the right words to say
Thinking of a way to get out of this misery
So head over heels about you
Way too shy to tell you of my admiration for you
And how much I truly likes you
Is one of my mind greatest mysteries
Wandering in realm confusing my fantasies with realities
Wishing I was a conversationalist
To have you speechless and blushing
With rhythm and rhyme
But that reality is so far out of reach
But I hope physically, lyrically,
emotionally and romantically
This poem says what's on my mind

HER GRACEFULNESS

Your immaculate beauty has capture every man's eyes on the street
Everything that you are and possess says made in heaven
Your outer finesse has no flaws, no faults, nor imperfections
A true goddess is what you are
Those sparkling brown eyes melts my heart without a heat
Your sunbeam likened smile mesmerize
Your lips are so desirable like something dripping with chrome
Such a temptation to kiss
Your curves are just an unframed masterpiece
You're the moon with such perfect shape
Captivating are your long sexy legs and alluring thighs
The way you walk like sprang in your hips
Got my eyes stuck on you
Your gracefulness completely takes my breath away
You're an epitome of beauty that extends into the heavens.

LOVE OF MY LIFE

The very thoughts of you makes me nervous
You got me feeling as light as a May cloud
Pulsating like a summer brook
Hot like twelve o'clock in a Caribbean July
My eyes light up every time I see you
I get butterflies whenever you speak
You angelic voice so sweet and intimate
Whenever we hug I don't want to let you go
Whenever we kiss you melt my heart
before the kiss is complete
Without a heat
Your scent the perfume of night-blooming flowers
So irresistible sweet
Nothing in my life before we met means this much
You are my will
My satisfaction
The love of my life and my joy concoction
Your spirit
Your essence
Your listless ways
Your serenity
Your passion
Your kiss
Your touch
Your love
They engulfs me more than the whitest snows.

ENDLESS POSSIBILITIES

You are the answers to all my riddles in life
My every dream come true
My one and only true love
Let's explore and discover
The wonderful and endlessly possibility of us two
Let's run away together
I don't care where
It doesn't matter, as long as we are together
England, Netherlands or even Disneyland
Where ever is fine by me
I just don't want to be away from you
I had no idea when we met I would fall
so helplessly in love with you
Never in my life could I have ever in my wildest dreams
and indefatigably fantasies imagined being in love
In a way that was completely indescribable by words
All my life I look for a girl stunning and beautiful
But never expected those unsurpassable impossible
to not only be met but miraculously surpassed.

The reality of poverty hits like Mike Tyson fist
It took so many innocent soul with it
And leave others broken with their shoulders
falling down like teardrops
Fearful of going forward and equally fearful of turning back
The race of Black men are suffering
A journey fill with uncertainty
Our ancestors lived a painful history
We now understood the shameful past
Today while we have move on from the past
The more things remain the same
The drums are beating
The tempo are compelling
The voices are echoing
The message is out and equality is the sound
The rhythms will never change
Until equality leaves it high holy temple
And comes into our sight to liberate us into life
Until courage strikes away the chains of fear from our hearts
Until freedom breaks the shackles from our feet
Until the barriers of injustice broken down
Until race discrimination fell to the ground
Until the souls of ancient, historian of pain rises up
The rhythms will never change
The beat goes on
Keep marching forward
Change must come.

Love can makes you feel high as a May cloud
But can also makes you feel low as a morning mist.

Love is real like a heartbeat
Like volcano it flows unapologetic
It has no barriers
It has no motives
It has no fear
Always arrives at its destination
Whether to heal a broken heart
Or brings happiness to an empty soul.

LOVE FOR HURT

It's like we are playing a game of love for hurt
The more I love you is the more you hurt me
I lost the only game that I couldn't play
Love hurts more when you're in it
It took the very heart of me
Without even an apology
Nevertheless I'm still in love with you
I have always love you more
I was destined to
The love I have in my heart was meant
To be from the start
I was always yours to have
But you were not mine
And destined to love me not
I lost the only game I couldn't play
You hurt all the love away
Without a care in the world
Do you like to see me broken?
With my shoulders falling down like teardrops
Saddened and blue
Along way down on every sides
Trying to fill this empty hole you left behind
I got nothing else to lose
I guess our love is lost
Just memory of how it use to be
Maybe just when I taught I was a winner
I lost the only game I couldn't play.

The love of my life how I adore thee
Beautiful and amazing
More gorgeous than even the portrait of Mona Lisa
More delectable than anything my eyes ever behold
Lips so soft and red
To kiss them I ponder
Your eyes are so stunning
They sparkle like the stars in the night sky
Face that's so mesmerizing and errorlessly made
Your curvaceousness, lustfully excite both body and mind
Skin so smooth and spotless
You are delightfully beautified with humor, style and grace
Your valiant walk and the refined swing of your hips
Hypnotized me with gracefulness
Someone so breathtaking is such a pleasure to behold
Words just aren't enough to say
I wish I could pause the time so this enamoring scenery never ends
Such an insightful and marvelous reflection of poignant empathy.

ALWAYS ON MY MIND

In your thoughts is where I want to be
When you close your eyes
I want to be the one you're thinking of
My mind go crazy when I don't hear from you
And even when we are apart
Your voice moves me and brings me tears of joy,
A sound I've never before known
Thinking about you, makes me constantly smile
Something deep inside tells me you are the one
There is no one else I would rather have by my side
Because there is nothing more wonderful
Than having you here in my arms
I would do anything just to be with you
Each day and night you prove my life worth while
I appreciate you so much
You're someone I adore
This insatiable feeling for you is so incredible,
I want it to hold me captive eternally
I carry your heart with me, so deep inside forever
Anywhere I go, you will go too
How amazingly sweet it is that you are always here
Warm and cherish in my heart.

UNTAMED BEAUTY

You are an untamed beauty and the mystery of life
That I wanna know all about.
Everything about u is splendid
Like a thornless rose without compare
Your mesmerizing face
Your sublime look
Your infectious ways
Your delightful smile, your succulent lips,
your marvelous eyes, your personality
Your intelligence
What can I say?
You are the perfect blend of sweetness
A woman whose beauty knows no measure
If there was a law for being too sweet
You would definitely be arrested
You are the prettiest,
Drawn in by pure angelic I can't help but to stare
I have never seen anything so astonishing
If I had to invent a new word,
I would call you the "beautifullest"
Like a Hollywood spotlight shining of glorious treasure
You melt my heart with every scene
Elegantly and effortlessly you take my breath away
The way you walk like you're on Broadway
Dazzle me like a magical sunset
You are an epitome of beauty
From your hair follicles
All the way down to your toenails
God's most stunning creation artistically,
creatively and breathtakingly,
handcrafted to perfection

A masterpiece of an unframed portrait
You are rare as Madagascar vanilla
More priceless than Africa's most precious gems
You're every man's lust and schoolboy's greatest fantasy
The princess every king want to crown
You deserve a throne.

Like strawberries on ice cream
You melt my heart with sweetness
I crave your touch
I crave your tenderness
I crave your lips
I wanna kiss them so passionately
Like they are going out of style
I worship your body I don't think I can get enough
You make my body ravenous with hunger for you
This immense desire for you overpowered me
Like the forbidden fruit in the Garden of Eden
Let me explore your every curves
And discover all your hidden treasures
I'm sure what is yet to be discovered will enlighten
My very soul.
And I will rejoice and sing your praises
Allow me to gaze at the gate of your femininity
Where "mhmmm" and "aahhh" meets
Exploring your most sensual parts
Drinking honey the from your pink walls
Meeting your
Crowning points between my lips
Slithering every inch of you
Like a scavenger
It's gonna take hours before we are through
All your desires will surely be fulfill
I'm so addicted by the essence that's wonderfully you.

BLACK QUEEN

Phenomenal woman
That's me
Well-rounded, thick, slim, voluptuous and full figured
"Take a glimpse and be amused"
The glow of my chocolate skin
The sun of my smile
The grace of my style
Phenomenal woman
That's me
Sexy, fluffy, beautiful and proud
Such diversity in my skin tone
Dark, chocolate brown, macho brown and honey brown
My body is exquisitely curved
Don't need sexy lingerie or fishnet pantyhose
To capture a man's attention
They swarm around me,
Like a hive of honey bees
Phenomenal woman
That's me
"I'm naturally beautified"
Bless with everything to spare
From my hair follicles to the sole of my feet
What you see is neither an illusion nor a delusion
It's a stunning gift of natural beauty from god
The span of my hips,
The curl of my lips
The swing of my waist,
And the joy in my feet
The inner mystery hidden between my thighs
Phenomenal woman
That's me

Gods crowning achievement
"A symbol of eloquence"
The integrity of a great woman
That's me
By far the most attractive
My curvaceousness,
Full breasts, hips and thighs
My sexiness can never be quantified
The way I walk
Like I got gold mine hidden
Between my indulging thighs
The captivating swing of my hips from side to side
The way my dress holds me, envelopes me,
imprint me, teases my skin like the wind
The harmonious movement of my feet
Got your attention like Miss Universe,
I realize the reason why God created me
For everyone to see
I'm full figured, beautiful and proud
Phenomenal woman
That's me
Everything I am
You are not
Boldness with a purpose
I proudly wear the crown
Black, beautiful and proud
Phenomenal woman
That's me.

I never thought I could find so much happiness
My life is so enriched by you that I can't help but smile
You are simply amazing
Each and every time I see you
My heart leaps for joy
It's the way your eyes sparkle like diamonds
The way your smile shines
How gentle and comforting your touch is
How encouraging your words are
True beauty only exists,
In your wonderful presence
You are by far the most beautiful being
My eyes have ever seen
Every time that I am with you,
You give me the feeling of peace and tranquility
Whether we are
Just basking in the moment of something spontaneous
Magically and new
Or just talking about the plans we have
For us two
There is a million reasons why I can't love you enough
Words don't even come close to expressing
How much I truly love you
You are the best thing that has happened to me
I could never imagine a life without you!
I love you with every breath that I take
No matter where I go, what might wanders my eyes
Or what I'm doing, you're always on my mind
You are the other half of my heart
Every day with you is a dream come true
I am so lucky to have you in my life
Thank you for being my everything.
I love you.

GODDESS

Some say God have made all women beautiful
Others say beauty is in the eyes of the beholder
But when I look at you, you defies all definition
fitting the description of beauty
You have succeeded all of my known comprehension
You are perfect in every way imaginable
You must be a goddess
Your outer finesse has no imperfections
You are the breathtaking reflection
of God's heart, unfathomable and pure
Words just not enough
I'm trapped in a box of wonders
You test every limits of my imagination
A stupendous glory of God's finest work of art
It's as if you carefully crafted
by Jesus craftsmanship to perfection.

I'm so blessed I found you as my priceless prize
You are a treasure in every way
I searched with the rest and discovered the best
Meeting you was my luckiest day
Your tolerance is endless
However I choose to be
Having my love makes you happy
So you just keep on loving me.
That's why, my boo bear, whatever else I do,
One thing is for sure
No matter what
I'll just keep on loving you.
You are my perfect partner
Sweet lover, trusted friend
That's why my thoughts of you comes so frequently
They are always fill with incredible, amazing, special,
wonderful and unforgettable moments of you
I never thought that I could spend each precious minute
loving just one special person
And find so much happiness within it.

There's something really special about you
My eyes light up every time I see you
So pulchritudinous, symmetrical and glamorous
Completely mystified and lost for words
Such vision of pure celestial
So eye-catching, beautified and errorless
Made in heaven by God's finest work of art to perfection
Your skin is as soft as flowers petals
Face that mesmerize
With a smile that makes my temperature arise
Legs so thrill it would mute any men
Sparkling brown eyes dazzle me with
Scintillating indigo
Lips so desirable like something dripping with honey cone
Your curves are such an unframed masterpiece
A goddess in every way, shape and form
An idol of astoundingly philanthropic
Adorable in every way imaginable
Your face is what every magazine wants to put on their front page
Paparazzi dying to photograph you
Even Picasso would struggle to paint such flawless imagery
Your incomparable beauty defies all definition known to mankind
Even the angels in heaven gets jealous of you
Never has such remarkable beauty seen here on earth.

HURT

Since you took your love away
I haven't seen the light of day.
My whole world turns gray
I can't stop my tears from falling
Forcing a smile as I blink the tears away.

I lost the only woman I ever love
You broke my heart into pieces.
Choking on my loneliness confused at what to do
Wondering how I am going to get through the day.

My life is a total wreck when I'm not with you
Drowning in the memories of yesterday
The pain continues to this day.

A love so strong could not be wrong
Yet someone took you away from me
You both play me like a game.

What should have last an eternity
Now it's just memory of what use to be
When will this pain go away?

My love for you was so plain to see.
It was written all over me
But in return you took the very heart of me.

I am letting you go without any fuss.
It's the way you wanted it to be
Nice and quiet while I struggle to keep my dignity.

Goodbye, my Princess.

SUCK IT UP

Life is hard and the road is rough
The feeling is tough
Sometimes it's hot
Sometimes it's not
The wind blows through singing trees
All around is instability and chaos
People busy going about their business
Old folks drinking coffee
Chatting about ancient, historian of pain
A shameful past
Children playing tirelessly without a care
What bittersweet
The mist has gone
Leaving only distance memories
Like a spinning wheel of steel
On old cotton fields
Woven into threads of fabric
No hush or crutch
You better push and puff
Through the hustle and bustle
Oh what, bittersweet
Orange sun ray begin to claim
The sky and on distant hills
Evening has come
Got to take a nap
Before dawn blind
To the sky its appearance.

ON A MISSION

I was born a dreamer
I have not only exceed all expectations
But also vacillation my doubters and critics
I was born without limitation or boundaries
The greatest pleasure in life is doing
What people say you cannot do
Sometimes while you are busy doubting yourself
Others are intimidated by your potential
Always go above and beyond people's expectations
Make yourself distinct
You are rare never be afraid to be seen or heard
You were born with an immeasurable soul
Prepared to tackle obstacles with courage and confidence
Never give anyone the power to determine your worth or value
There are no limits to what you can accomplish
Except the limits you place on your own expectations
No one can make you feel inferior without your consent
Always be the best version of yourself
You are the architect of your own future
You will never be the person you are destined
To be with limited imaginations.

Some say circumstance and distance makes the heart ponder.
Others say out of sight is out of mind.
Distance may matters to the mind but heart don't care
What we have is so special
It doesn't matter the distance or changes of seasons
You could be in Amsterdam, Netherlands,
England or even Disneyland
Our love will last beyond the test of time
I don't care what people say
I'm gonna love you through life's challenges and criticism
Our book of love has no end or beginning
But continues evolves like the universe.
Bonded to you in emotional bliss, united in physical rapture,
rich contentment and total fulfillment
You brought to me
I'm happy you chose me from all of the rest.
You means everything to me
I hope we never break apart, because I'm in love with you
Words simply can't describe
My feelings for you,
A connection that is so true.
In at least a thousand ways
Whether it be a thought or a moment that we've shared
It only takes a second to get me find here to there
Thinking such wonderful thoughts of you.
Truly amazing I never thought
That I could spend each precious seconds
Thinking about just one special person
And find complete happiness within it.

LOST FOR WORDS

You are the essence of my being
You captured me with your presence
The elegance of the specimen was heavenly sent
You are a host of perfection
Like soul food for both body and mind
Delightfully you make all my senses smile in awe!
A goddess
Your divine ways and qualities surpass that of an Angel
Can't take my eyes off you like a predator stalking its prey
Your temptation is my only demise
You are my disease and my only remedy, addicted to you
My seductive sinister
Enchanted me with your delightful thighs
Hypnotized me with your beauteous eyes
Bound me by your gracefulness
Entice me with your pleasure
Captivated me with your intelligence
Intoxicate me with your scent
Seduce me with your flirtatiousness
Lures me with your lips of affection
I've become a victim of my own rapacious desire
Slave to the rhythm of this unquenchable lust
It burns uncontrollable like wild fire
There's no vulgarity in me when I say
You are perfect in every form and proportion
Mesmerized and infatuated by you
Intrigued and lost for words
Every time I look at you.

Life is like the ocean
You have to learn to flow with its tides
You will never get to your destination being faint-hearted
You can never cross the ocean until you have the courage
to lose sight of the shore
You can never soar above the clouds until
you have the fearlessness to lose sight
of the ground
You have to remember even eagles have to learn how to fly
The power of your belief is everything
Never underestimate it
The potential for greatness lives inside you
Never limit yourself
Limitations are for people without confidence
So learn from your failure and embrace the lesson
Your attitude and desire for success determines
your direction
Never lose your focus
The true essence of living is about discovering
your passion and creating yourself
Focus on your dreams and set new goals
The vision of your mind will give you a clear view
into life's future
Respiring clouds of doubts
with dedication and passion will give you
the strength and desire
to rise above endless mountains of fear.

MUSIC OF THE HEART

Trust your intuitions
Only your heart can tell you what is right
So listen its beats
Follow its rhythm
Understand its lyrics
Know its highs, lows and in-between notes
Each notes has a soundtrack of its own
Listen closely to its melody
Memorized its tunes
Let every breath harmonize and synchronized.

The real integrity of a man is to develop
an attitude of gratitude
A true sense of accountability
Always live with the consciousness
that your actions will affect others
Always be an inspiration and a role model
to those around you
Your mental mindset is everything
So be a reflection of what you need to see in others
You will never be a true leader
without the right mindset and dedication
Your limitations is only a lock of your imagination
No one can makes you feel insignificant
without your consent
Never lose patience
Be true to yourself and have the courage
to face life with boldness
You can accomplish anything
with the right mindset and principle
Start thinking of yourself as a genius
Sometimes the biggest hurdle is the decision to act
Your passion for success should always
be greater than the fear of failure
When you are confident in yourself
you also demand the confidence of others
Practice values and always think highly of yourself
In the end you will never be anything more than
what you perceive yourself to be.

THINKING OF YOU

In the morning before the sun rises
Anticipating the ray of sunshine peeping through my window
As I watch you helpless getting last mins of sleep
Breathing slowly, completely at peace

Thinking of you
When the first ray of sunshine comes over
The distant hills and glaze the valley with warmth
As you gently arose from your sleep
Looking so beautiful like silvery dew on a sunflower

Thinking of you
At midday when the sun is hot like a Caribbean summer
When the heat is pulsating and the stress at work is overwhelming
The thoughts of your smile, your cheers, your hugs and kisses
Create a feeling that is impossible to express with words

Thinking of you
In the evening when work is through
And the anticipation of coming home to you running wild
The need to touch you, feel you, kiss you is almost
Too much to hold inside

My thoughts of you comes so frequently
Even at midnight in the silent hour of the night
When the moon and stars brings me peaceful dreams
My mind is on you

You are so precious and my wishes for you are endless
You mean everything to me
My entire universe

The beam of light in my darkest hour
My strength when I'm weak
My support when I both fail and fall
You are everything that keeps me grounded in this world.

PARADISE PLUM

Many are my favorite things
But nothing is more precious than you are to me
My most treasured and cherished
My crown jewel
You are nothing short of magical and breathtaking
A woman of such high standards, class and gracefulness
You are brave, bold, beautiful, talented and intelligent
I never chased perfection but I pray I'm your perfection
Let me love you through Jesus's perfection
You really makes me understand the truth of his grace
Because you are the reflection of his heart
The rarity of the specimen has been heavenly sent
I can feel the glow of your blessings
The way I feel connected to you spiritual
And at the same time incredible attracted to you physically
Like my religion, you bring so much joy and meaning to my life
Like heaven in all its essence
Your whole being is beautiful
God created you in his excellency
You are comparable to an angel so divine
How incredible thankful and bless I am to have you in my life.

The scent of the specimen has been heavenly sent
Like Madagascar vanilla
Every time I smell your irresistible and intoxicating scent
I absorb it
The essence that's wonderfully you.

LOVE DON'T LOVE ME

Some say falling in love is the most beautiful thing
Others say love is infectious
You cannot pour it on others without getting
A few drops on yourself
But I wish I could say the same for you
Oh how you play me
You use me
You deceive me
You drained my very soul
Love how you deprived me of you
And left me broken
For so long I have searched
Looking for you and when I did found you
For a brief moment you had me on a high and then
you push me off the edge
Like a cold-blooded killer
You exceed all expectations of cruelty
You took the very heart of me
Today I say goodbye to something
That I wish was permanent in my life
Love you have cost me too much!
How can something so beautiful bring
So much pain and sadness?
You have rob me of my innocence
You have blinded me
From finding my soul mate
Only left me broken hearted and with shattered dreams
But I will not be defeated by love
Fear well to next time
Love you cost me too much!

COMFORT ZONE

Take a step out of your comfort zone
Stop playing hide-and-seek with yourself
If where you are in life doesn't feel right in your heart
And if what's in your heart doesn't feel right in your life
You need to change the direction and focus of your life
Sometimes our biggest hindrances is the echo
of our own fearfulness to act
Instead of embracing our own imperfections
We are dead silent in our disappointment
Blaming ourselves for all the wrong reasons
Instead of relentless in pursuing our goals, dreams and aspirations
We are busy focusing on how we are seen and judge by others
When you clearly don't need the approval you're seeking
Self-control and self-empowerment is strength
Learn to master your emotions
It's the calmness of your thoughts that conquer the storm.

UNRECOGNIZED

The fear of not being recognized
I fool myself thinking I was expressing
My story in my poems
I was lying to myself
Neither was I being heard nor be seen
Chasing an American dream living in a Caribbean is surreal
The scariest part is the realization
that you have lost yourself completely
I was only living
But my existence wasn't being celebrated
I felt like a fatherless child
A constant clouded mind with still no sign of guidance
An uncertain path, a traumatic past
Unwanted by a society dark with cruelty
The dream destroyed, but I will not be defeated
Essence burdened with deep depression
The guilt upon society and the ignorance so wrong
Such a fool thinking that I can change the world with my poems
Just another empty soul looking for ways be heard
There's no voice for the voiceless
Free will and freedom of expression is just a distant dream
Everything you say get filtered through the lens of others
You'll be judged on everything you do even by the clothes you wear
It's all about propriety in this troubled world
Living with such uncertainty of time.

A unframed masterpiece

Like brilliant round diamonds
Every curves of your body perfection is sustained
Not even a sculpture craftsmanship can't imitate
You are gorgeous like Mona Lisa come to life
Astonished eyes all stare
You demand all men's attention
The whole world surrender to the magnificence of your being
The rarity of your beauty does not have rivals
It's the world's greatest treasure
There are no words to describe
How beautiful she is
How special she is
How amazing she is
Her smile sparkle like precious gems
Her angelic eyes glow like candle in the night
Her face admirable like an eclipse
Her body is modernly engineer to perfection
It's almost impossible to capture in language
Her beauty extends into the heavens
Even the great Shakespeare would struggle trying
To find articulate words to describe her incomparable beauty
Picasso is bless with enormous talent and gift still wouldn't be able
To paint a portrait of such flawless ,unframed masterpiece
Not even scientist can't explained such
remarkable beauty here on earth.

LOVE

A fool for love is a fool for pain
Maybe I win, maybe I lose
I pour my heart into love
But you were never mine to have and destined to love me not
Love
You had me on a high and then push me off
the edge like you wanted me to die
I have been broken by
Love
Dust from a heart of flame
I have been forsaken by love
Laughter turn into tears
I have been played by love
I bet and lost it all
Love
I have been taken for granted by love
It's scary thinking I could lose you forever
Love
So hard to leave it all behind
But today I say goodbye to something that
has been very permanent in my life
Love
I am tired of writing poems about you
Love
But I will not be defeated by love
As I attempt to stage a new love affair, a destined romance
These eyes are open for love
I will not be intimidated by love
These arms are open for love
I refuse to stay broken by love
This heart is ready for love
I'm so elated these gates are open for love
Fear well to next time hurt and pain
Love.

THE TAPESTRY OF LIFE

Sometimes what appears to be the end may
actually be a new beginning
Keep reminding yourself that everything happens for a reason
You can control how you survive it
Forget the unnecessary but always remember
every good deed on your journey
Life is about discovering your authentic self
and enhance each opportunity given
Accepting hardships as the pathway to growth
Every obstacles in life is a lesson
Focus on your goals and never lose your direction
You are the driver of your own destiny and
the captain of your own ship
you can navigate yourself in any direction you choose
It will eventually take you to a destination
Never lose your focus
The power of your ability is everything
Be true to yourself and have the courage
to face adversity with boldness
Your ambitions should drive your passion
and your determination fuel your appetite for success
The true essence of greatness is about discovering your talents
and finding your purpose in life
Learn to master your strength and minimize your weaknesses
Your confident will reflects your credibility
and also determine the level of confidence others have in you.

POVERTY

Today I say goodbye to something that has
been very permanent in my life
The mist has gone and the message is out and poverty is the sound
It's the most common crime throughout society
Usually hidden by the high and mighty
The guilt upon society and the ignorance so wrong
Never has life struggles more real
While billionaires with money they can't spend
The dream maybe destroy but I will not be defeated
The echo will never change
Until success leave it's high towers on Wall Street
and comes into our lives to liberate us out of poverty
Until equality leaves it's high holy temple and brings us justification
Until success reaches the four corners of the earth
The message will never change
Fear well to next time poverty
Success I am so elated about you.

Milton Keynes UK
Ingram Content Group UK Ltd.
UKHW010939221123
433051UK00003B/203

9 798888 103326